THE GREAT CLASSROOM COLLAPSE

Teachers, Students, and Parents Expose the Collapse of Learning in America's Schools

by Lance Izumi

THE GREAT CLASSROOM COLLAPSE

The Great Classroom Collapse
by Lance Izumi
July 2024

ISBN: 978-1-934276-55-6
Pacific Research Institute
P.O. Box 60485
Pasadena, CA 91116

www.pacificresearch.org

This book is dedicated to the memories of Marion Joseph and Janet Nicholas, who fought valiantly for effective reading and math instruction.

&

CONTENTS

INTRODUCTION

"There is no accountability in education," observed California mom Rebeka Sinclair, and "it shows you the institutional brokenness that can occur when debate is stifled, when no one questions narratives, or holds anyone accountable."

How broken is education in America?

On the 2022 National Assessment of Educational Progress fourth-grade reading exam, 66 percent of students taking the exam failed to achieve at the proficient level.[1]

The results were even worse on the eighth-grade reading exam, with 69 percent of students taking the test failing to demonstrate proficiency.[2]

According to a NAEP reading report, "At the fourth grade, the average reading score was lower than all previous assessment years going back to 2005," while, "At eighth grade, the average reading score was lower compared to all previous assessment years going back to 1998."[3]

In mathematics, proficiency rates were also painfully low.

On the 2022 NAEP fourth-grade math exam, 64 percent of students taking the test failed to score at the proficient level.[4]

On the eighth-grade exam, the bottom fell out. A shocking 73 percent—nearly three-quarters—of eighth graders taking the test failed to demonstrate proficiency.[5]

The NAEP math report stated that the 2022 results showed the largest decline in scores "in NAEP mathematics at grades 4 and 8 since initial assessments in 1990."[6]

"A lot of these kids are coming out of high school with a fifth-grade reading level," said former longtime California teacher Christy Lozano. "They can't go to [community college] and make up for that," she observed, "and so they're super depressed."

It is no wonder that students are depressed when they discover that they have not been taught core skills effectively. The consequences turn out to be severe.

According to the National Council on Teacher Quality, "Students who are not reading at grade level by the time they reach fourth grade are four times more likely to drop out of high school, which in turn leads to additional challenges for them as adults: lower lifetime earnings; higher rates of unemployment; a higher likelihood of entering the criminal justice system; and a greater chance of needing to access government benefits to meet their household basic needs, such as food and heath care."[7]

Yet, parents and their children are often deceived because of rampant grade inflation in schools.

For example, from 2010 to 2022, the grade point average in English, math, science, and social studies courses among students taking the ACT college-entrance test increased, while their ACT scores decreased in every subject.[8]

As math education author Doug Lemov has noted, "It is no surprise that national data from the ACT show high school students' grades rising—a majority of college test-takers now report receiving an A in each subject—even as their achievement scores have stagnated or declined."[9]

The question then is why are students around the country achieving at such low levels in core subjects such as reading and math?

This book seeks to find out the answers to that critical question. Only by identifying the reasons for poor student performance can solutions be crafted to raise the learning levels of our children.

Those reasons are varied and range from schools prioritizing equity and social justice concerns over equality of opportunity and meritocracy; to teaching methods and curricula unsupported by empirical evidence; to teacher training programs that fail to instruct prospective teachers on what really improves student learning; and to bureaucratic adherence to failed education programs.

In this book, readers will meet students, parents, K-12 teachers and tutors, college instructors, and policymakers who are experiencing the collapse of learning in America's classrooms and who are fighting to change things for the better.

Among the people profiled is a mom who grew up in the tiny West African nation of Sierra Leone and who has fought against the efforts of her school district to decrease the rigor in her children's school in the name of equity.

There is also the high school junior who remembered that in her elementary school "the core academics were not too challenging in any sort of way," and, as a result, she had to use an online supplemental program to help her in math.

There is the Georgia mom and former teacher who revealed the shocking deficiency of her teacher education and the tragic consequences for her students.

There is the Oregon teacher who is bucking her school district in order to teach reading effectively to her students.

There is the California mom who revealed the poor reading instruction in an expensive private school.

There is a top engineer at the famed Jet Propulsion Laboratory who has fought against the failed reading and math curricula at his children's school.

There is the California math tutor who is seeing students from an affluent school district struggle because of ineffective math instruction.

There is the college instructor who detailed the appalling lack of math preparedness of his students.

But there is also the California state legislator, the daughter of immigrants from Mexico, who is pushing to ensure that children receive the foundational reading skills they need to succeed, which gives hope that much needed reform can be achieved even in states where failed pedagogy has been entrenched for decades.

Indeed, research on what actually improves the learning of children is being used by parents to force change and, as Rebeka Sinclair has observed, "We're seeing a huge shift take place across the country."

Through personal stories and data analysis, this book details the battles and the shifts going on in schools across the nation. In too many places in America, learning in the classroom has collapsed, but it can be improved so that our children have a greater opportunity for a successful future.

SECTION ONE:
THE EQUITY AGENDA AND THE COLLAPSE OF MERIT AND RIGOR

CHAPTER 1
Equity and the Classroom Collapse from a Student's Viewpoint

"I didn't speak English until I was about four years old," says Charlotte, who is now a 16-year-old public high school student in California. Charlotte's name has been changed in this book for privacy.

The daughter of an immigrant mother, she said, "my mom spoke Swiss German to me because she is Swiss." Her father is "an ABC—American-born Chinese," so he "spoke Mandarin Chinese to me."

According to Charlotte, "my grandparents on my father's side were actually both born in China, but because of issues with Communism they escaped to Taiwan."

Both her parents are musicians. Her father plays the viola in a string quartet, while her mother plays in a piano duet and teaches piano.

Her parents have a strong belief in the value of a quality education. "They definitely believe in hard work, applying yourself, and to being smart about how we use our time," she observed.

"Education is one of the most important things and they have done well in providing us with good support structures," she said.

While she has been blessed with supportive parents, Charlotte has not been as lucky with the schools she's attended.

She says her public elementary school "was definitely very safe and created a lot of space for creativity." However, it was a different story when it came to academic learning.

"The core academics," she noted, "were not too challenging in any sort of way."

She started having problems in understanding math, so her father introduced her to the acclaimed online Khan Academy. Started by software developer Sal Khan, the Khan Academy produces thousands of free video tutorial lessons on a wide variety of classroom subjects and topics.

According to the organization, "Khan Academy offers practice exercises, instructional videos, and a personalized learning dashboard that empower learners to study at their own pace in and outside of the classroom."[10]

In addition to math, which was Charlotte's problem subject, Khan Academy tackles "science, computing, history, art history, economics, and more, including K-14 and test preparation (SAT, Praxis, LSAT) content."[11]

Importantly, says Khan Academy, "We focus on skill mastery to help learners establish strong foundations."[12]

The Khan Academy program has proven very successful for many children across America and around the world.

One analysis of more than 1,000 Khan Academy-using students in fourth grade to seventh grade in a school district in Pennsylvania found that during the 2017-18 school year students using Khan Academy for just 30 minutes per week were "more than 2.5 times as likely to meet state standards with a score of proficient or advanced compared to students who used Khan Academy for less than 15 minutes per week."[13]

For her part, Charlotte says that Khan Academy "became a very big help in mainly my math at that time." She started using the Khan program in the second grade and after that math "became very, very straightforward and easy."

If it was not for the supplemental help she received through the Khan Academy, Charlotte believes, "I would probably have struggled a lot more in middle school a bit and definitely in high school."

Specifically, she recalled, "In elementary school and middle school they definitely went over the big [math] concepts, but Khan Academy gave more details and a lot more example problems and their videos are really good at explaining." In fact, "Sometimes I thought it was better than how the teacher explained it."

Many other states, including California, use the controversial Common Core national standards in math, which were adopted in the early 2010s. As *The Washington Post* notes, "Instead of memorizing procedures to solve problems, kids are asked to think through various ways to arrive at an answer to explain their strategies" as the program is "designed to promote a deeper understanding of the subject and help students make lasting connections."[14]

The paper quoted one academic proponent of Common Core who urged that success in math should be redefined: "It's not being able to tell me the answer to three times five within a heartbeat. Rather, being successful means: 'I understand what three times five is.'"[15]

Yet, the ivory tower theorizing behind Common Core means little to students like Charlotte who cannot understand why math is being made more confusing for them.

Regarding the Common Core-aligned math textbooks her school issued to her, Charlotte said, "A lot of the textbooks that we used in mathematics in elementary school had us do a lot of explaining, but most of the time we actually didn't know how to explain and sometimes we had to explain things where it was more like a 'yes' or 'no' answer."

Common Core also emphasizes visuals. For example, the *Post* described how an array is used to teach multiplication:

An array...is a model that students can use to master multiplication. It's essentially a grid. Students can plot out 5 x 6 by coloring in five rows of six or six columns of five. Count the total number of squares and you've got the answer: 30. Break the grid apart into sections, and you can see three sets of 10. The visual representation can also help kids understand area and measurement and can plant the seed for connections that will help in later math.[16]

For Charlotte, however, "visual aspects that were supposed to help us learn personally made it more confusing for me."

Middle school presented a whole different set of problems for Charlotte.

"Middle school was definitely a lot more chaotic," she said, with students exhibiting "a lot of behavioral issues." As a result, "there was definitely a downfall in the amount you can learn because there were more disruptions and the teachers had absolutely no control."

Charlotte's siblings were also impacted by the disruptions at the middle school. She described the experience of her older sister:

My sister, who is now in college in Pennsylvania, had a specific situation where every day there was this one kid who had behavioral issues and it came to the point where the teacher was really just unable to teach. And several times the whole class had to leave the classroom because there's a rule that the security guards cannot physically touch students. So it made it so that when they wanted to learn they would have to move to another classroom in order to learn anything, and then leave that one student to stay. So it was a very complicated procedure and it really stalled how much they could learn.

These disruptions continued in high school.

For instance, Charlotte said, "we had numerous fire alarms that went off due to smoking, which always sets off the fire alarms, and those were very disruptive to class."

"In fact," she said, "my [Advanced Placement] World History exam got interrupted by a fire alarm, which was a very, very big hassle and very hard on all the students that were taking the exam because that meant they had to choose between turning [the test] in as is or retaking it, which many didn't want to do."

Such disruptions have real consequences. Research has shown that disruptive students have a negative impact on the learning of their fellow students.

According to a study by researchers at the University of California at Davis and the University of Pittsburgh, leaving disruptive students in a classroom has "a statistically significant negative effect on their peers' reading and math test scores."[17]

In addition, a single disruptive student "also significantly increases misbehavior of other students in the classroom," causing them to commit 16 percent more infractions than they otherwise would.[18]

The researchers conclude that their findings "provide strong evidence of the validity of the 'bad apple' peer effects model, which hypothesizes that a single disruptive student can negatively affect the outcomes for all other students in the classroom."[19]

In order for students to learn they must have an environment conducive to the learning process, and if schools fail to provide that environment then they are failing at one of the reasons for their very existence.

Teachers fully understand the consequences of not addressing classroom disruption.

For example, Christy Lozano, a former longtime California teacher said: "I could see all the behavioral stuff. I know how much the administration did not support teachers. You have to have a safe classroom and you have to have classroom management in order for kids to learn. You can't have kids hijacking the class all the time."

Disruptive behavior by her fellow students, though, was just one of the challenges that Charlotte had to face in school.

In middle school, Charlotte experienced a noticeable and pronounced lessening of rigor in the school's academic practices.

The first thing she noted was the lowered expectations that teachers seemed to have for students: "I think they definitely cared about how we did in our classes, but that didn't make them push harder." Rather, even when the school wanted students to do better, "it's usually the teachers going easier on us, instead of us getting pushed harder."

How did teachers' "going easier" manifest itself in the classroom?

"It was easier to get high grades," said Charlotte, "and teachers would be more lenient offering second and even third chances."

Specifically, she cited multiple opportunities offered to take tests or turn in homework.

The lessening of requirements and the ease in getting high grades is a phenomenon not restricted to Charlotte's middle school.

Former longtime Los Angeles teacher Larry Sand, who is president of the non-profit California Teachers Empowerment Network, pointed out that nationwide 29 percent of eighth graders are proficient in reading and 26 percent are proficient in reading based on scores on the 2022 National Assessment of Educational Progress exams, yet, "grade inflation is at epidemic levels."[20]

For example, Sand noted that in Los Angeles, his former district, more than eight out of ten sixth graders received passing grades in spring of 2022, despite the fact that only a little over a quarter of sixth graders in the district met or exceeded standards on state and national tests.[21]

When it came to high school, Charlotte saw the same reduction in academic rigor, starting with the way students were admitted into the school.

Historically, the school, which is a public school, admitted students based in significant part on an entrance exam and was highly regarded. Charlotte's oldest sister, who attended the school, had to take the test.

However, when her next oldest sister applied to the school, the test had been eliminated and the admissions criteria changed to incorporate factors such as grades in middle school and completion of an application essay.

When it came time for Charlotte to apply to the high school, the admissions criteria changed again to a lottery system. In other words, pure chance would determine if a student was admitted to the school or not.

Why would a high-performing public school change its admissions policy so dramatically? Answer: to advance the neo-Marxist Diversity-Equity-and-Inclusion social justice agenda, which puts a premium on ensuring equity as opposed to equality. In this case, equity meant having a student body based on racial proportionality rather than a student body where all applicants, regardless of race, had the equal opportunity to be admitted based on merit.

Charlotte was fortunate because the school retained a sibling preference criterion, so she was admitted. "However, a lot of my friends didn't get in and they were very sad about that," she observed.

The reaction of Charlotte's friends underscores the fact that despite the progressive equity mantra, aspects of education such as admissions are a zero-sum game. There are a finite number of spots in selective schools and changes to admissions criteria benefit some students, while disadvantaging others.

When Charlotte saw how the change in the high school's admissions criteria would negatively impact students who had worked so hard to prepare themselves for admission into the school, she spoke up at one of the webinars that the school district conducted to elicit community input regarding the admissions change. She wanted to "speak up for a lot of my classmates and friends saying how it's unfair."

However, she was shocked when another speaker said those attending the high school were either white supremacists or Asian.

Despite her opposition, the school board changed the admissions criteria to a non-merit-based lottery system. Charlotte saw the negative impact of this change immediately.

In her freshman classes, she recalled, "the amount of rigor went down because teachers had to adjust to the students."

"There were less academically motivated students so the teachers had to adjust to that."

As a result of the new lottery admissions system and the lower level of student academic preparedness, teachers "became more lenient." For instance, deadlines became fuzzier, with teachers adding grace periods. Teachers offered "more test retakes and more curving of test scores." "They really increased the extent to which they did that compared to when my older sister was here," observed Charlotte.

Despite the lessening of classroom requirements and rigor, students still failed courses. Charlotte noted, "actually my grade set a record for the number of students that failed classes." Further, "the year below me broke our record in the number of students that failed courses."

So how did teachers at her high school become more lenient and less rigorous?

Charlotte recalled her honors chemistry teacher telling her that in previous years he would go over a set of topics. However, when she took the class from him he did not cover as much material.

According to Charlotte, the reason the chemistry teacher fell behind in covering topics was due to the deadlines he set for assignments, which were not met by many students, "so we actually couldn't cover as much content, which he kept mentioning." She said, "that made me realize, 'Oh, wow, I guess we are really moving slowly this week.'"

Because the lottery admissions system lowered the performance level of students attending the school, Charlotte observed a noticeable impact on how much material could be covered in class:

But based on what I've seen in the class, the participation is very, very, very low. So it dragged on the class a lot. [The teacher] would ask for volunteers to answer questions and there's always a pause or there's always a delay in the question being answered, even when he called on someone. So I realized that all these little pauses here and there really add up because at the end of class he didn't actually finish what he wanted to say.

"He was trying to accommodate more to what the students were capable of," she said, "so there wouldn't be as much failure" when it came to deadlines and grades.

For her part, Charlotte felt that she was held back "because a lot of times we had to go over problems that he went over already," so "we just spent time going over that rather than learning new content."

Science was not the only area where Charlotte felt shortchanged by her public school education.

Her middle school had gotten rid of eighth-grade algebra. The Common Core math standards which California uses pushed algebra from the eighth grade to the ninth grade. However, Charlotte said that her goal was to take geometry in the ninth grade, which meant that she had to take algebra in the eighth grade. Because her middle school had eliminated eighth-grade algebra, "we had to take an online algebra course that we had to pay for."

"If you wanted to get ahead," she emphasized, "then you would have to pay for an online course instead of doing it for free in eighth grade [at public middle school] because they got rid of it." And the reason why the school district got rid of algebra in the eighth grade was because of supposed equity.

"They just wanted everyone to be on the same level," she said, "but the issue is that when you put everyone on the same level you're restricting those who have the potential to go ahead." Further, even when algebra is delayed to the ninth grade, "in those classes, it might still be difficult for those who need extra support, so it just becomes very messy."

If math was not good at her schools, then English was worse.

"So nobody likes English [at her high school]," noted Charlotte. "Nobody enjoys it and there's a lot of unnecessary work, like sometimes even baking, but a lot of work that's not even actually analyzing, writing, and learning vocabulary."

Because there was little emphasis in her high school's English writing classes on writing and writing support, there was a domino effect in other classes.

For example, in her history classes, she said, "You do feel a big struggle at first because you're not used to writing so much, and you're not used to analyzing the literature so much." In order to make up for students' English-skill deficiencies, "somehow those history classes actually kind of turn into English classes."

It was not just in classes like history where poor teaching and the consequent impact on students' English skills manifested themselves. Lack of a proper foundation in English, said Charlotte, "made it more difficult, especially as students decide to take the SAT, which has a big English section." She observed that, "a lot of my classmates always do better in the math section than in the English section."

The school district's purposeful decision to dumb down her high school, through equity-inspired policies such as taking merit out of the admissions system, caused demoralization among teachers.

Charlotte noted that when her school went to a lottery admissions system that "a lot of teachers left" because many of them "felt that this was a step backwards."

Also, the principal resigned saying, according to Charlotte, that he wanted to "apply his passion for education in a district that values its students and staff through well organized systems, fiscal responsibility, and sound instructional practices." While the principal couched these reasons as "pathways to equity," Charlotte observed, "the type of equity that he [supported] sounds different from what his school board had in mind."

Why is Charlotte's experience so important?

First, what she went through is representative of what is happening at schools around the country.

Second, Charlotte is a high achieving student. Many people think that lowered standards in the public schools only affect average or low-performing students. However, as Charlotte's experience indicates, lowered standards can have important adverse impacts on highly talented students.

Finally, the fact that Charlotte attends a public high school that had a reputation of excellence, yet is failing all of its students, shows that the problems of K-12 public education are widespread and are not confined to just stereotypical low-performing schools.

CHAPTER 2
Equity and the Classroom Collapse from a Parent's Viewpoint

"I was born in Grand Rapids in Michigan," says Minnesota mom Oredola Taylor, but "my parents were both immigrants from Sierra Leone." Her amazing life story would greatly affect her view of education.

Located on the west coast of Africa, Sierra Leone is situated next to Liberia and Guinea. "It's a beautiful place," said Taylor and she wistfully recalled that it was referred to as "the Athens of West Africa because it had one of the first universities and very high standards of education."

Her parents both came to the United States for college and met at Washington, DC's Howard University, one of America's top historically black colleges and universities. Although she was born in Grand Rapids, she was sent back to Sierra Leone when she was a very young girl when her parents divorced.

"I grew up in Freetown," she recalled. A former British colony, she said, "once the British freed the slaves" they "would capture slave ships and would free the people in Sierra Leone."

The original Black settlers of Sierra Leone, she said, "were actually African Americans who fought with the British during the Revolutionary War" because "the British promised them freedom." When the British lost, the Crown eventually offered to send many of these African-American Loyalists to Sierra Leone.

Because of bitter disputes between her parents, Taylor had a childhood filled with turmoil, going from relative to relative in Sierra Leone. Then, she was hidden by her father with relatives in England before being taken by British authorities. Ultimately, she was reunited with her mother, who then took her back to the United States.

"So, pretty traumatic," she recalled.

During her time in Sierra Leone she said, "I wasn't a good student because I didn't have the best instruction, but the whole importance of education was always instilled in me."

Once back in the U.S., she grew up in Houston, Texas. She experienced prejudice and discrimination, but from a seemingly unlikely source.

In middle school, "even though I was coming from Africa, I had to deal with a lot of prejudices between African Americans and Africans."

"I had a lot of issues with African American students and teachers," she said. "I would be asked whether I lived in a tree, just insulting me as an African as if my family and I were backwards and didn't wear clothes."

Her best friend was Korean. "She was a Korean immigrant and hardly spoke English," she said, "and I was from Sierra Leone, still trying to figure my way, so we became good friends and we're best friends to this day."

"A lot of my friends were immigrants—Nigerian Americans, Jamaican Americans, Korean Americans, and a lot of Vietnamese people," she said.

Her high school "was an all-Black school" and "math was my biggest struggle." "So at this all Black school there was a white teacher who took me aside and I met with her pretty much every day after school," she remembered, "and that's kind of how I became an engineer."

"I didn't like math and I wasn't very good at it," she said, "but I was a hard worker."

She eventually received her undergraduate degree in mechanical engineering from Oklahoma University and then two graduate degrees from the University of Wisconsin, one in mechanical systems engineering and the other in entrepreneurial management. She now works as a product development expert and holds a U.S. patent on how to make documents difficult to counterfeit. She is a true American success story.

Taylor is now a single mother of three boys and lives in St. Paul, Minnesota.

Still, despite family challenges, she says: "It's not easy. I'm divorced. I'm a single mom. But you also have to be the chief educator."

Therefore, "I was always involved in [my sons'] education."

She discovered the French Immersion School, a public school that was, at the time, one of the best schools in the St. Paul school system. The school was run by a Nigerian American, plus many teachers were immigrants from African countries such as Cameroon, Togo, and the Ivory Coast.

From having excellent STEM courses to having a Ph.D. music teacher, Oredola said that the quality of the education program at the school was high and noted "they always were number one or two for science and math."

Yet, despite the history of high student performance at the school, things started to change, and not for the better.

In spelling, memorizing spelling rules was jettisoned and "kids were now being told to spell as it sounds, so whatever you want, the way it sounds."

But, French and English use different sounds in their languages. "So there was a huge confusion," she said, "and I remember [my children] not able to spell anything because of mass confusion."

Math instruction saw similar negative changes. The school had previously used the well-regarded Saxon math curriculum.

According to the *Smarter Learning Guide*, Saxon math uses a spiral method of math instruction "that combines incremental skill development with ample practice to achieve better practical math results than standard curricula."[22]

Further, compared to most math programs in public school systems, "Saxon Math uses a much more back to basics approach to teaching math, emphasizing math facts and strategies, as well as lots of individual practice and drill, as opposed to group work and creative or unconventional problem solving methods that are taught in many reform math based programs."[23]

She liked Saxon curriculum, but "that all went out the door."

As a result of the change in math curriculum, she had to resort to supplementing the instruction her children received at the school.

She said, "My oldest son was doing well, but I had to enroll him in the Kumon afterschool math program. I also hired a math tutor to help the kids with math and they just were not getting the instruction from the classroom."

And it was not just her and her sons who were having newfound math learning difficulties after the changeover in curriculum.

"A lot of immigrant parents from India, Somalia, and Nigeria all go to Kumon."

"After school," she noted, "you see immigrant kids, the first generation kids, packed in there because the parents have to supplement what they're not getting from school."

In addition to the changes in reading and math, she lamented, "the Ph.D.-level musician who was teaching violin, piano, drumming, you name it, she was gone."

"I just saw this as an assault on the things that made the school successful being taken away," she said.

She also cited lax grading policies as a problem at the school. "Especially during COVID," she said, "you didn't have to show up; you could just surf; you could do pass-fail; you didn't have to have a letter grade."

Perhaps the biggest change came in the area of discipline. The school had a significant minority student population and most of staff members, including the principal, were Black. Discipline policy changes occurred because of equity concerns, she said, but the result was "things just started to fall apart."

She recalled "one situation where a kid brought a knife and threatened another kid," and the perpetrator was "back in class, maybe the next day." She emphasized: "This was an elementary school."

The loosening of discipline policies caused teachers to leave the school. "I remember one teacher moving to the Waldorf school, a private school, to teach there," she said. Shaking her head, she said, "these were really excellent teachers."

She also made the important point that even if "it's just a few kids, it just breaks the spirit of the entire classroom." "That whole discipline thing," she concluded, "it was a huge one."

All of these developments greatly upset the parents at the school, who were very involved in school life. "We're not necessarily wealthy," she said, "but we would raise funds to bring interns from France and Senegal or wherever to come work with our kids."

"This wasn't money from the schools," she noted, "so the parents were very active."

"So when we started seeing all of these things happen," she recalled, "we started protesting and showing up at the school board." Then, she eventually came to realize that the dumbing down of her children's school was done on purpose.

When parents confronted school district officials, they were told "that the school was privileged; we were too privileged; and we needed to be like everybody else." In other words, equity trumped excellence.

Because the French Immersion School succeeded in raising the achievement of minority and immigrant students, it undercut the diversity-equity-and-inclusion narrative that systemic racism is the reason for poor performance among historically underserved children.

Ironically, it did not matter to district officials that the protesting parents were racially diverse, with many from immigrant backgrounds. She said that the district had to destroy the school because it undercut the progressive narrative on the achievement gap: "If you have a school where kids are achieving, it was just too inconvenient. So that's why they targeted that school and made sure to run it into the ground before they were done."

Part of the reason for the dumbing down, she believes, is that there is more government funding for remedial programs than for high-performing programs. But, she also said it "was also dumbing down students, propagandizing students, and creating racial division."

The result of the dumbing down of the French Immersion School was hugely disheartening for her.

Previously, "everybody knows the Frenchies" because "those kids are just brilliant." Teachers in middle and high school liked the Frenchies "because they were more respectful, more disciplined, and more hardworking."

"But that's because the fundamentals were placed in them."

Sadly, "It's no longer the case in French Immersion." The school had "fallen so far down that it went from having a waitlist of parents trying to get in to where nobody had any use for it."

"Because the school had fallen so far because of district policy changes and because of the COVID pandemic, I finally had to pull my kids from public to charter," she said.

Yet, even the charter-school option was not free from the district's heavy hand.

"They didn't want people escaping to charter school," she said, "so they came with an agenda and got the charter schools going down the same road." She ended up choosing private school for her two younger sons.

The bottom line, she observed, "when you have a poor start as a child, it's like a curse that keeps on giving, so it's really important that you give your child the fundamentals even if you have to send them to a private school."

In fact, she said, "I know of people that said to me, 'I graduated from high school thinking I was doing good, go to just even a community college and have to do remedial, and now it's costing me how many thousands of dollars just to catch up on stuff that I thought I knew.'"

"The grade inflation is not helping you for sure," she warned. She believes there is systemic racism in education, but not in the way that progressives believe. "The systemic racism is the current system that makes Black kids not achieve, and then the assumption that Blacks have no agency and if you don't help us we're not capable." She emphasized, "So that to me is the racism because there's nothing wrong with us."

Having seen firsthand how ideology and self-interest trumped the needs of children, she bitterly concluded, "The school system is a huge money laundering operation."

In St. Paul, "kids are walking out there who can't read," but "everybody's getting their cut—the unions, the administrators—it's a crazy money laundering operation and the taxpayers are paying out the nose for these kinds of results." And the ultimate insult, "they have the nerve to say let's keep this going and blame racism."

She mused about the incentives in public education saying: "So if you're not going to get paid unless 90 percent of your kids are proficient and then all of a sudden they'd be doing whatever they have to do to get those kids proficient in math. But if you get more money because of failure, then I'll get more for failure."

This cycle of failure means, "I need more money to do the same or worse and that's the way the system works right now."

The impact of the failures of the public schools ripples through American society. "I have friends who have businesses and they complain that they cannot find [competent] people," she said.

What would she do to correct America's failing public education system? "So it's not that complicated to fix this, we could start tomorrow," she said. "Change the incentives," she observed.

She is now on the board of a private micro-school. Micro-schools, which are small learning communities that often have mixed-age student populations and innovative and customized curricula, are often viewed as a halfway point between private schools and homeschools.

Taylor advocates for empowering parents with choice options in education and forcing the public schools to compete and meet the demands of their consumers. "Give me my money, give me the money, the money that I'm paying for my kid to go somewhere [other than the public school]," she urged, and "that competition will, believe it or not, fix the public school system in no time."

"If educating kids is what pays then that's what will happen," she concluded, "but if it's mis-educating them that pays then that's what will happen."

SECTION TWO:
THE COLLAPSE OF
READING SKILLS

CHAPTER 3
Reading Instruction: What Works

"I was getting students in high school," said former veteran Virginia high school English and journalism teacher Shelly Norden, "that if I asked them to pick out an adjective or an adverb in a sentence, they couldn't do it." She observed, "writing was in big decline and reading, too."

The students in her classroom were no anomaly. The reading proficiency of students nationally is at record low levels.

Why were the English skills of students in Norden's school and schools across the country cratering? To answer that critical question one must look at what the research evidence shows regarding effective and ineffective reading instructional methods.

Years of research has shown which instructional methods are effective in teaching children to read.

The National Reading Panel, which was established by the federal government in the late 1990s, reviewed more than 100,000 studies on reading and selected the most rigorous of these for analysis, concluding that the best approach to reading instruction incorporated:

- Explicit instruction in phonemic awareness
- Systematic phonics instruction
- Methods to improve fluency
- Ways to enhance comprehension.[24]

In a comprehensive 2023 report on the quality of reading instruction in America, the National Council on Teacher Quality stated: "More than 50 years of research compiled by the National Institutes of Health, and continued through further research, provides a clear picture of how skilled reading develops and of effective literacy instruction. These strategies and methods—collectively called scientifically based reading instruction, which is grounded in the science of reading—could dramatically reduce the rate of reading failure."[25]

Further, "research indicates that more than 90% of all students could learn to read if they had access to teachers who employed scientifically based reading instruction."[26]

What, then, are the elements of this scientifically based technique that has been proven to be successful and holds out so much promise for the nation's struggling readers?

The NCTQ report noted that are five major components to the science of reading:

> Elementary teachers need to understand and know how to explicitly and systematically teach the five components of scientifically based reading instruction, including: (1) mapping students' awareness of the sounds made by spoken words (**phonemic awareness**); (2) systematically mapping those speech sounds onto letters and letter combinations (**phonics**); (3) providing students extended practice reading words with learned letter-sound combinations so they learn to read words with automaticity, without a lot of effort, at a good rate, and with expression (**fluency**); (4) building word knowledge using student-friendly definitions and

engaging practice opportunities (**vocabulary**), a skill closely associated with the final component; (5) ensuring students have the skills, knowledge, and strategies to understand what is being read to them and eventually what they will read themselves (**comprehension**).[27]

"All students," said the report, "especially struggling students, need explicit systematic teaching of literacy (including phonemes and letter-sound relationships), practice, student-teacher interaction, carefully chosen examples, decodable text, and feedback that corrects their errors."[28]

It is critical that teachers "understand and know how to teach all five components of scientifically based reading instruction" because "of the interconnectivity of these components." A teacher "who lacks an understanding of one will be less effective teaching the others, and students who miss instruction on one component may struggle to become fully literate."[29]

It is therefore highly troubling and revealing that the NCTQ found that 75 percent of the college teacher preparation programs it surveyed failed to address all five components and a shocking one in four failed to address adequately any of the five components.[30]

No wonder then that a major review of reading instruction research by education researchers at the University of Alabama found that low student reading achievement could be traced to "teachers unsure of the most effective practices and how to use them effectively in a classroom setting and context."[31]

Equally concerning is the NCTQ's finding that four out of 10 teacher preparation programs "are still teaching multiple practices contrary to long-standing research, which can undermine the effects of scientifically based reading instruction."[32]

Among the practices that are contrary to scientific evidence are instructional methods such as balanced literacy, the three-cueing system, readers' workshop, and leveled texts. These anti-evidence-based practices will be defined and discussed in detail in the ensuing chapters in this section.

As the NCTQ noted, "No medical school would ever teach aspiring doctors using practices known to be ineffective, yet these practices remain all too common when preparing elementary teachers to teach reading."[33]

Yet, despite phonemic awareness being the foundation upon which the five pillars of the science of reading rests, it "is consistently the least addressed component" in teacher preparation programs.[34] Indeed, 65 percent of teacher preparation programs fail to address phonemic awareness adequately.[35]

Given these appalling deficiencies, it comes as no surprise that a majority of the teacher preparation programs surveyed by the NCTQ received either a D or F grade.[36]

The parents, teachers, and policymakers profiled in this section will reveal how ineffective reading instructional practices and policies manifest themselves in the classroom, how they impact real children, and what can be done to ensure that every child receives reading instruction that is based on science.

CHAPTER 4
Former Teacher Reveals Reading Failure

When parent and former teacher Missy Purcell realized that she had been using failed instructional methods to teach reading to her students, searing questions burst into her mind: "What have I been doing? What did I do? Who did I fail? Who is failing my kid or other kids? Why didn't I know this? Was my [education] degree worth anything? I just felt angry."

Like Saint Paul on the road to Damascus, she thought she had been doing the right thing for years until that moment when she had her epiphany and understood that she had actually been part of America's reading problem, not part of its reading solution.

Growing up in an old farmhouse in the foothills of the Appalachian Mountains in a small town in Northeast Georgia, she always wanted to be a teacher.

"I wanted to be a teacher since I was a little girl," she said, "so I would teach my dolls." "I had a classroom in my bedroom," she recalled, and would beg her teachers for leftover copies of textbooks "and I would teach those all summer long."

She laughed saying, "I had a library in my bedroom with card catalogues, just like a future teacher nerd in the making, that was me."

She went to public school and then attended the University of Georgia. She loved learning and, no surprise, got her degree in middle school education.

While at the University of Georgia, "I learned all about this way to teach writing and reading," which had all the hallmarks of the reading instructional method called balanced literacy.

For years, balanced literacy has been popular among progressive educators. It is characterized by a variety (some would say a mish-mash) of components. According to a report by the National Council on Teacher Quality (NCTQ):

> Balanced literacy models represent an approach to reading characterized by the use of read-alouds, shared readings, small group guided reading, and independent reading, typically relying heavily on leveled books and focusing on meaning-based instruction. In contrast to structured literacy, balanced literacy models often eschew the explicit, systematic teaching of phonemic awareness and phonics skills, demonstrating a preference for approaches emphasizing context clues, like three-cueing.[37]

NCTQ says that under three-cueing reading instructional approach, "children who encounter a word they do not recognize are instructed to use one of three strategies: 'guess what the word might be' based on context; 'look at the picture to help guess what the word might be;' and 'look at the first letter to help guess what the word might be,' and if the guess makes sense, then check to see if it 'looks right.'"[38]

In other words, instead of sounding out letters and connecting them to make a word, this three-cueing method encourages children to guess as to what the word might be. Yet, as the NCTQ study points out, "Despite widespread use by K-2 and elementary special education teachers, reading experts discourage guessing techniques because they represent lost opportunities to help children practice decoding [i.e., pronouncing], and represent an ineffective strategy for reading advanced texts."[39]

"What I didn't get," she said, "were true standard skills that you need to teach kids—foundational skills."

A federal report on evidence-based foundational reading skills recommends students "develop awareness of segment of sound in speech and how they link to letters." Linking sounds to letters "is necessary to prepare [students] to read words and comprehend texts." Giving students this ability "to isolate sounds and then link those sounds to letters will help students read about 70 percent of regular monosyllabic words, such as *fish, sun,* and *eat.*"[40]

The federal report also recommends that educators, "Teach students to decode words, analyze word parts, and write and recognize words."[41]

"Once students know a few consonants and vowels," the report states, "they can begin to apply their letter-sound knowledge to decode and read words in isolation or in connected texts."[42]

The federal report illustrates this decoding/pronunciation method called "Sounding Out," which includes speaking the letter sounds and then combining them into a word such as "hat":

> Teacher: How does this word start?
> Student: /h/
> Teacher: Then what's the next sound?
> Student: /a/
> Teacher And then what sound comes next?
> Student: /t/
> Teacher: What happens when you put
>   them together?
> Student: /h/ /a/ /t/
> Teacher: What is the word?
> Student: *Hat!*[43]

Shockingly, Purcell said that she never learned decoding techniques in her teacher education program at the University of Georgia.

"I didn't even know the word 'decoding,'" she said. Neither was she taught the terms, "phonemic awareness and just basic sentence structure and fluency."

Journalist Emily Hanford, in a widely cited overview of reading instructional methods, observed:

> Balanced literacy proponents will tell you their approach is a mix of phonics instruction with plenty of time for kids to read and enjoy books. But look carefully at the materials and you'll see that's not really what balanced literacy is mixing. Instead, it's mixing a bunch of different ideas about how kids learn to read. It's a little bit of whole word instruction with long lists of words for kids to memorize. It's a little bit of phonics. And fundamentally, it's the idea that children should be taught to read using the three-cueing system.[44]

In her early teaching career, Purcell loved the balanced literacy approach and idolized one of its celebrated academic proponents—Lucy Calkins.

An education professor at the prestigious Teachers College at Columbia University, Calkins pushed a balanced literacy curriculum that was adopted in schools across the country from California to New York.

According to the education publication *Chalkbeat*, under the Teachers College-balanced literacy model, "Teachers typically deliver 10 minutes or less of a mini-lesson such as how to find a text's main idea." Then, they "send students to fan out, often curled on a classroom rug, to choose books at their own reading level," while teachers "shuttle between children to check on their progress, either individually or in small groups."[45]

Chalkbeat noted, however, "research shows that reading is generally not a natural process that children can pick up independently and that explicit lessons to help students sound out words are essential." Unfortunately, these phonics-based lessons, which the federal report said were critical in building the foundational reading skills of young children, were either not part of balanced literacy programs or only haphazardly included in inadequate amounts.[46]

No wonder, then, that Missy graduated with her college education degree, but said, "I lacked a lot of the knowledge."

In fact, looking back at her experience in college, she said, "How did I not know this was not a good thing?" Sadly, she reflected, " But when you're in college, you think the people educating you are the experts and that they're presenting you with published authors who are the experts."

Yet, "I was not taught how to teach kids to actually read—the foundational skills part—when I was in school and I wasn't even taught to how to identify those kids [who could not read] or to notice red flags about those kids."

"There was very little to help me even notice that the kid might be falling through the cracks," she recounted, "and you would think that the leading state school in my state that's charged with producing the future generation of educators, who are going to influence future communities, would have a little bit more interest in ensuring that we were giving our kids the skills they needed."

As a young acolyte of Calkins and her balanced literacy instructional method, Purcell enthusiastically carried the torch for the method in her classroom.

"I actually ended up becoming the observational classroom for other schools to come and see," she said. "I trained other teachers and I went to other counties and trained them to set up reading and writing workshops in their classrooms."

Reading workshops are part of the balanced literacy approach that, according to the NCTQ, are "characterized by read-alouds, small group guided reading, shared readings, and independent reading."[47]

This program lacks "systematic and explicit instruction in all foundational skills," and, like other balanced literacy models, "uses cueing systems for solving unknown words, encouraging students to focus on initial sounds of words and meaning cues rather than explicitly teaching decoding strategies."[48]

She said of the method: "I call it 'limp through a book.'" Students would "look at the first letter," but then, "look at the picture" and answer: "Is that really happening? Is that really that word? Did that make sense?"

"When I was working with low-level [reading] kids," she said, "they were reading books with pictures, which is a little embarrassing when you are in the fifth grade, and even in middle school that was the case."

While proponents of balanced literacy would make superficial nods to the importance of foundational skills like phonics, she details the reality in the classroom.

She said that while there was supposed to be "a little bit more of the foundational skills in the classroom, that was not my reality because I didn't have any tools that I was given by my district to teach foundational skills."

Instead, "I was praised," she said, for "embracing the reading and writing workshop."

What turned the Lucy Calkins balanced-literacy approach into classroom reality was the curriculum called Fountas & Pinnell, which has been used by many school districts throughout the United States.

In her highly influential podcast on reading instructional methods, Emily Hanford, observed:

> Balanced literacy is another name for what Calkins and Fountas & Pinnell and others have been selling. There's not a precise definition of balanced literacy. But what I've learned in my reporting is that in schools that say they do balanced literacy, you're very likely to find Lucy Calkins and Fountas & Pinnell. And you're almost certain to find those leveled books . . . The

basic idea with leveled books is that if kids are moving up levels they're learning how to read.[49]

Irene Fountas is a professor at Lesley University in Massachusetts and Gay Su Pinnell is a professor emeritus at Ohio State University and are, as reported by Emily Hanford and Christopher Peak in the respected investigative news outlet *APM Reports* from American Public Media, "authors of some of the most widely used instructional materials in American elementary schools, and their approach to teaching reading has held sway for decades."[50]

Hanford and Peak said, "The center of the controversy are teaching techniques to use context, pictures, and sentence structure, along with letters to identify works," which the outlet noted, "is a theory about how people read words that has been disproven by cognitive scientists."

Fountas and Pinnell write:

> The goal for the reader is accuracy using all sources of information simultaneously....If a reader says "pony" for "horse" because of information from the pictures, that tells the teacher that the reader is using meaning information from the pictures, as well as the structure of the language, but is neglecting to use the visual information of the print. His response is partially correct, but the teacher needs to guide him to stop and work for accuracy.[51]

Cognitive scientists who have been studying and reporting on how young people learn to read well were appalled. Mark Seidenberg, a University of Wisconsin-Madison cognitive scientist, told Hanford and Peak:

> If a child is reading 'pony' as 'horse,' these children haven't been taught to read. And they're already being given strategies for dealing with

their failures. This is backwards. If the child were actually given better instruction in how to read the words, then it would obviate the need for using all these different kinds of strategies.

. . . They illustrate they still don't get it and that they're still part of the problem. These folks just haven't really benefitted much from the ongoing discussion about what are the best ways to teach kids to read so that the most kids succeed.[52]

"There's no question that [Fountas and Pinnell's approach is] making it harder for children to succeed," said Seidenberg. Sadly, "You get reports of children who finally do succeed at reading with this kind of one-hand-tied-behind-your back sort of approach but hate it because it was really onerous."[53]

The Fountas & Pinnell curriculum received a failing grade from the widely used and cited evaluation by the non-profit education organization Ed Reports. Among the deficiencies in Fountas & Pinnell's K-2 curriculum is a lack of "research-based or evidence-based explanation for the teaching of phonological skills" and a lack of "research-based or evidence-based explanation for the sequence of phonics."[54]

In particular, "foundational skills lessons [such as phonics] are recommended for 10 minutes a day, which may not provide sufficient time for students to receive daily explicit instruction to work towards mastery of foundational skills."[55]

Also troubling, "Since Letter-Sound Relationships and Spelling Patterns lessons do not span the entire year, students do not have daily opportunities to practice decoding sounds and spelling patterns."[56]

Problems continue in Fountas & Pinnell's curriculum for later grades. For example, in the curriculum for grades 3 through 5 there is limited instruction of phonics, word recognition, and word analysis. Also, like in the earlier grades, only 10 minutes a day is allotted for foundational skills.[57]

Further, assessment materials provided by Fountas & Pinnell "do not clearly inform instructional adjustments of phonics and word recognition to help students progress toward mastery, and many assessments are optional."[58]

One of the aspects of Fountas & Pinnell, as Hanford noted, is the use of leveled reading material. Purcell had a huge library in her classroom and the books "were all leveled by letter, so I helped kids figure out their letter by giving a little oral reading test and then I would assign them a letter and that's kind of where they camped out for most of the year."

She would tell parents at what level their child was reading, which she said made her feel good. The idea is that as children move up the letter scale it would indicate that their reading was improving. At least that is the theory.

In reality, she said, "I had no idea why they moved there, other than I moved them there."

"Really, honestly, I had no idea why kids were up the letters," she recalled, "and what that meant."

As the Ed Reports evaluation of Fountas & Pinnell's fifth grade curriculum stated, the letter system for complexity makes little sense because the "methodology for placing students in texts for independent reading or for group instruction does not ensure students are reading complex text and may not provide adequate support for students to ensure adequate growth towards mastery of the standards for their grade level."[59]

The bottom line was failure for too many of Purcell's students.

A common frustration for her was finding out that after all her teaching, "I have kids who can't read, who can't write complete sentences, and I'm supposed to be teaching them how to write a story or an essay or a persuasive writing piece, and they can't even write a sentence."

When her students were supposed to be reading independently, "all the time that kids were by themselves was wasted instruction time." Indeed, it was like random galaxies spinning off into the universe:

> I felt good, right, because I had a checklist, a mini-lesson, an anchor chart, [independent reading], and they were doing it because I

taught them how to do it, or they looked like they were doing it. I was there meeting in small groups, I had my checklist of who's working on what, everyone in my room was reading something different, they were all writing something different. It was so overwhelming sometimes to keep up with who's doing what, who's getting better, who's not getting better, who needs what. Some kids just couldn't write a complete sentence. So I just had pages of endless connected words and no punctuation, capitalization, nothing. I didn't even know where to start to help them.

She had fifth graders reading second-grade-level books. "I was frustrated a lot," she said, because when these fifth graders were able to read those second-grade books, "I'd put an A in the grade book, but I've always felt that was misleading because they were in the fifth grade."

Ineffective reading instruction caused students to have poor reading skills, which in turn caused them to not reach their full potential as adults.

"I always get emotional when I talk about this," Purcell said, "because I can tell you the names of kids just about every year that I taught that couldn't read and I always wonder where did they end up?"

"I have found some kids on Facebook that I taught," she revealed, "and I can tell you there's one girl who doesn't have a job that's making a lot of money." She wondered, "Did I play a part in that?"

"I didn't help her," she lamented, and "she left fifth grade and went to middle school and she couldn't read."

"I had a little boy that was French Canadian that moved here and it was his first year in my fifth-grade class," she remembered. "He couldn't write complete sentences," she said with emotion, "and he just went to middle school and he could not write a complete sentence." With remorse she said wistfully:

"I wonder what happened to him. I just wonder. I didn't have what I needed, so I couldn't do what I needed to do."

Because so many children had problems reading under the balanced-literacy approach, parents were often pushed to read to their children more after school. Purcell, though, pointed out that this shifting of the teaching burden was unfair to non-English-speaking parents. "How are they supposed to read books in English with their kids," she noted.

When she was teaching she had a large group of children from the war-torn Kosovo region of Southern Europe. "They didn't speak English," she said, "so I was trying to balance content at the same time as we were learning to read, but they weren't getting foundational skills, and their parents wanted to help but couldn't." Some parents "might be working three jobs and they can't always sit down and read with their kids at night."

"I went to school and I was being paid to teach them these things," she emphasized, "it's my responsibility no matter what."

"I wasn't empowering [parents] to do anything different than what I was doing," she said, and "looking back, it was like the definition of insanity—doing more of what's not working."

She taught for a decade and "then I left and raised my kids." It was when she sent her kids to school that the scales started to fall from her eyes.

She took a class on reading instruction and was fascinated because the teacher "taught me the word 'decoding' and the 44 phonemes." Phonemes are the sounds that letters make. "I made flashcards for all the 44 sounds that we have in the English language and I learned them all," she said.

Of her three children, all of whom went to school in the same district in which she had taught, her youngest son Mathew had the most difficulty reading. Matthew "did not learn all the sounds that letters make when he was in preschool." When he was assessed at the end of preschool and "they circle all the sounds they know, they circle all the letters," and she was shocked to see that her son "only knew the letter M for Matthew, so I knew something was wrong."

She noticed that things were missing from his instruction. He was missing "like a scope and sequence of basic skills to more advanced skills." Scope and sequence, in relation to reading instruction, is defined as:

> The scope and sequence used by your school should address the five components of reading (phonological and phonemic awareness, phonics, fluency, vocabulary, and comprehension) and encourage systematic, explicit instruction for learning how to decode words and how to comprehend texts. A scope and sequence should address all the elements of speaking, listening, reading, writing, and spelling that are necessary for most of your learners. It should include opportunities for daily, weekly, and cumulative practice and review across the grades. [60]

She said that scope and sequence starts with basic skills such as identifying sounds associated "with short vowels and then progress to teaching kids a few of the consonants and they build words." So, "if you know the consonants C and B you can say 'cab.'" Children learn C-V-C words, "which are your most basic words—consonant, vowel, consonant—then you later learn your long vowel words because those are made when you add that little magic E at the end." "So you learn these little blocks."

Students attach sounds to letters, she said, "and it goes from basic all the way up to your most high-level syllable types."

Scope and sequence, however, was not what her son received. In Kindergarten, she said, "Matthew was not advancing," so the school told her, "Read with my kid every night." "This isn't right," she thought.

Because she was a former teacher in the district and knew the staff, "my kid won the golden lottery ticket to go to Reading Recovery." Little did she know that Matthew's golden ticket was actually a lead balloon.

One description of Reading Recovery states that a session "involves reading familiar and unfamiliar books, with encouragement to guess from pictures, first letters and context." In other words, Reading Recovery's guessing strategy dovetailed with balanced literacy's "guess the word" approach.[61]

For Matthew, Reading Recovery was a disaster. "I hated it," she said, "because it was the beginning of my kid's road to reading failure."

She said that the Reading Recovery program "was supposed to be an intervention to help [Matthew] for 20 weeks, where your kid gets one-on-one reading instruction with this highly trained Reading Recovery teacher."

"The problem is," she said, "they are trained to teach kids to look at the first letter to see if it sounds right as they look at the pictures." While there is "sprinkling of phonics," there is "no sound scope and sequence."

Students are given a survey, but the survey "is not designed to screen for kids who might have true learning difficulties, maybe even be eventually diagnosed with dyslexia."

She said that Matthew "never should have gone into that program," and "when he failed to show progress after 10 weeks he should have been exited," but the school did not do that.

Based on Reading Recovery's evaluation system, Matthew "plateaued and they just kept doing it."

What Reading Recovery did was to teach Matthew bad reading habits. She said, "He learned to skip words and how to substitute words," and the program "ingrained in him these bad skills, which don't help you when you get into third and fourth grade and there are no more pictures and no more predictable books."

Predictable books use predictable word patterns "so they learn the pattern and they can look like they're reading," but when faced with a page of text that does not adhere to the pattern then children like Matthew fell off the rails and simply made up words. "He's actually using the same pattern to read words that weren't even on the page," she said.

"I got a paper," she said, "from his Reading Recovery teacher that told me to tell him to guess."

"Reading Recovery is literally balanced literacy in a one-on-one setting," she said, and schools "love it, they think it's great, they will stand by it, and they will fight you tooth and nail."

She noted that students going through Reading Recovery master the program, but "They don't master reading" because they "don't get the skills they need to apply to higher-level words."

Multisyllabic words 'are a nightmare, especially for kids with reading disabilities, and if they don't have those foundational skills mastered to automaticity that they can apply to a multisyllabic words later on, which is what their textbooks are filled with as they get older, then they just fall apart."

Her observation is borne out by recent longitudinal research.

Reporting on a landmark 2022 study by the University of Delaware, *Education Week* summarized: "Students who participated in the [Reading Recovery] program in the 1st grade had state reading test scores in 3rd and 4th grade that were roughly half a grade level *below* the scores of the student who had barely missed participating in Reading Recovery in 1st grade."[62] [emphasis added]

In other words, as students in Reading Recovery encountered more challenging reading material in higher grades, their performance declined significantly because they were no longer able to read the more difficult words.

Stanford University reading researcher Sean Reardon told *Education Week* that the study's "big takeaway here is that the estimated long-term effects [of Reading Recovery] are negative, significant, and meaningfully large."[63]

"What makes me mad," said Purcell, is "it's so expensive." "Think about it," she emphasized, "all schools have a one-person meeting and only a few kids get it." It is not surprising then that Reading Recovery is estimated to cost up to $10,000 per student, making it one of the most expensive reading intervention programs on the market.

When Reading Recovery did not work for Matthew, he was put into a resource classroom where he was taught using leveled-literacy intervention." According to Purcell, leveled literacy is "more of the same instruction, but now in a bigger group—the same method of instruction in a bigger group and also not as tightly controlled." No wonder she said, "they were hell bent on him staying on that same road."[64]

Eventually, she said, "I got a tutor [for Matthew]." Through the tutor she learned about the science of reading, which "I didn't learn in college." She started to look on the Internet and found:

> I was like, wait a minute, there's a whole group of me out there . . . I was reading teacher after teacher, and I literally started crying because this is me. Then your brain goes back in time, right? I just took a trip back to the past and that's when I was like, what have I been doing? What did I do? Who did I fail? Who's failing my kid or my other kids? Why didn't I know this? Was my degree worth anything? I just felt angry.

Besides using ineffective reading instruction for Matthew, the school was also giving misleading information about his achievement.

"The first grade teacher was giving him inflated grades," she said, "so he's looking like he's doing great, but he was failing every week."

By the second grade, "he's failing everything, I mean, he's just falling apart." He also started developing behavior problems.

It was Matthew's tutor, not the school, who taught him decoding skills. In fact, his second-grade teacher openly said, according to Purcell, "we don't teach them to decode."

Matthew is now in a special education class with an individual education plan. Purcell said that at that point he had not "been formally diagnosed with dyslexia, but the school psychologist said that he had the profile of a child with dyslexia."

The Mayo Clinic defines dyslexia as "a learning disorder characterized by problems identifying speech sounds and identifying how they relate to letters and words (decoding)." The disorder "is the result of individual differences in the brain that process language."[65]

The International Dyslexia Association warns that reading approaches such as balanced literacy "are not effective for students with dyslexia because these approaches do not focus on the decoding skills struggling readers need to succeed."[66]

Instead, the Association recommends structured literacy, which "explicitly teaches systematic word-identification/decoding strategies" and which "benefit most students and are *vital* for those with dyslexia."[67] [emphasis in the original]

KEY ELEMENTS OF STRUCTURED LITERACY

Key elements of structured literacy according to the International Dyslexia Association:

- **Phonology** (study of sound structure of spoken words) is a key element. Phonemic awareness (ability to distinguish/segment/blend/manipulate sounds relevant to reading/spelling) is central.

- **Sound-Symbol Association.** Once students develop phoneme awareness, they must learn the alphabetic principle—how to map phonemes to letters (graphemes) and vice versa.

- **Syllables.** Knowing the six syllable/vowel grapheme types helps readers associate vowel spellings with vowel sounds. Syllable division rules help readers divide/decode unfamiliar words.

- **Morphology.** A morpheme is the smallest unit of meaning in language. Studying base elements affixes help readers decode and unlock the meaning of complex words.

- **Syntax.** The set of principles that dictate the sequence and function of words in a sentence—includes grammar, sentence structure, and the mechanics of language.

- **Semantics.** Semantics is concerned with meaning. The Structured Literacy curriculum includes instruction in the comprehension and appreciation of written language.[68]

Yet, despite his apparent dyslexia, Matthew's school was not providing him with the structured literacy he needed, and instead focused on his supposed need for comprehension. However, Purcell said, the school did not understand that "comprehension is the product of being able to decode and your listening comprehension." The school was focusing "on the end result" and "missing what they had to do to get you there."

She started sending emails to the school saying that she did not want Matthew in this program, but the school was insistent. The COVID pandemic then hits, "the school shuts down and I can't get nothing."

In response, she ramped up the tutoring for Matthew. "It's not cheap to do this," she said, but the family put together the resources to make it happen.

When the school allowed students to come back for in-person instruction, she told Matthew, "You're not going back because they're not teaching you and I just didn't trust them." It turned out her mistrust was well founded.

When she sat next to Matthew for his virtual class, the teacher was teaching him reading using the guided-reading method, which is another balanced-literacy approach.

According to the NCTQ, under guided reading "students are grouped according to their 'reading level' and asked to read appropriately 'leveled texts.'" The method "typically promotes using cues (including background knowledge and pictures), English syntax, and visual information (including sound-symbol relationships)." Research shows that guided reading "is not as effective as explicit instruction, particularly for phonological decoding and comprehension."[69]

She was upset and sent an email saying, "When are you going to begin teaching him to decode? Where is he? What skills is he working on?" The response was, "Oh, we haven't gotten to that yet."

At the end of the fourth grade, Matthew continues to struggle. It was at that time that she got connected to a good lawyer who filed a complaint "basically for failure to teach my kids to read and using programs that were not evidence-based or aligned with what the [federal] Individuals with Disabilities Education Act spells out for kids who need this."

She ended up settling with the district. She said, "I can tell you that my kid went to the Sage School, which is a school for kids with dyslexia." Sage is "designed to teach kids using structured literacy" and everyone in the building is trained in Orton-Gillingham, which, according to its teaching academy, "is a direct, explicit, multisensory, structured, sequential, diagnostic, and prescriptive way to teach literacy when reading, writing, and spelling does not come easily to individual, such as those with dyslexia."[70]

Orton-Gillingham says that the five pillars of literacy include phonological awareness, phonics, (the ability to recognize letter-sound relationships in words), fluency (the ability to read with speed, accuracy and proper expression), vocabulary, and comprehension.[71]

It "is a highly structured approach that breaks reading and spelling down into smaller skills involving letters and sounds and then builds on these skills over time" and uses a "step-by-step process involving letters and sounds that encourages students to advance upon each smaller manageable skill throughout the process."[72]

Further, the approach "encourages students by seeing, saying, sounding, and writing letters to master decoding and encoding of words."[73]

For Matthew, this structured-literacy approach to reading worked. He entered the program not reading well, Purcell said, "And now he can write a whole story and he's working on a project right now where he's researching the country of Colombia."

"I'm just like, I can't believe it," she said. "That's so amazing."

Because his reading and writing improved so dramatically, he then did well in math, science, and social studies.

"What angers me so much," she said, "is that I shouldn't have to know these things for my kid to learn to read."

"We know that structured literacy works for everybody," she noted, and "it harms none and helps all." In contrast, balanced literacy "helps a few and harms a lot so why are they doing that?"

Looking back on Matthew's experience at the school, she said that so much of his time was wasted:

> My kid spent five years in a place where basically most of the text was inaccessible to him and he had to learn how to survive versus thrive. Instead of building upon skills, the gap was widening, not just with foundational skills, but also knowledge. Everyone was reading more and more complex topics and being exposed to greater vocabulary. My kid was often pulled out of read-alouds to get interventions. So he wasn't even having access to more knowledge. He was being robbed of that.

Sadly, she said that Matthew's greatest fear "was a spelling test," while his dream "was to learn to read."

"I hate this part," she said, because "I always get emotional." She lamented, "I thought that this is so incredibly wrong that we're systematically doing this to kids because people like a theory and they like their vibes-based teaching methods and it feels good."

"This is a harsh statement," she said, "but I don't really care how the adults in the classroom feel." Adults may feel good, but "it's robbing a kid of their life."

She said that she and her husband could not afford an expensive private school for Matthew, which doubly emphasizes why, "I thought this is wrong."

She is now helping other local parents with children who have dyslexia. She helps them get into the Sage School, and "it's like we're a little Underground Railroad of dyslexia."

"But it shouldn't take a person like me," she said, who "knows how to play the game."

Instead, "we need to take the money that you're training these special Reading Recovery teachers" and train teachers in "a method that actually works."

She ends on a positive note. Despite the years-long entrenchment of balanced literacy in her school district, she said with triumph, "our county is not going to use Reading Recovery next year."

"They're dropping it," she smiled, "which is huge."

Georgia lawmakers have listened to parents like Missy Purcell. In 2023, two state laws were passed that aim to promote instructional methods and materials based on the science of reading and structured literacy, with teachers trained or retrained in those methods by 2025.

CHAPTER 5
Oregon Teacher Fights for Effective Reading Instruction

"I definitely think kids are frustrated," said Oregon elementary-school teacher Kate Bowers. Specifically, children "are frustrated with reading."

The struggles helping children in the classroom are a far cry from the days of her childhood in rural Oregon when she would play teacher and teach her stuffed animals in a make-believe classroom.

"I'm one of those who always wanted to be a teacher," she recalled, "and I always knew that's what I wanted to do."

The daughter of a father in the construction business and a stay-at-home mother, she went to public school and then attended a small private college in Oregon where she received her teacher education. "We got good instruction on managing a classroom," she said, but little instruction in how to teach reading.

She explained, "It was assumed that since we knew how to read that we knew how to teach reading." "I don't feel there was really a whole lot of depth of instruction on how to teach kids to read," she said.

Basically, it was, "Oh, here's some good kids books and here's good children's literature."

She remembered, "I get out of college and I'm like, oh, I guess I'm going to have to figure out how to teach now." The victims of teachers' lack of preparation to teach effectively are, of course, the children.

"Kids have to wait for their teachers to learn how to teach well," she observed, "so, is that three years or five years?' During that time, children are receiving ineffective instruction that will stunt their educational development. Those are years of learning that children will never get back.

To the extent that her college had any kind of guiding reading philosophy, she said, "it was probably balanced literacy." She remembered having one professor who had taught in the public schools, "and that's what she knew."

Recall that balanced literacy is supposed to be a balance between progressive instructional methods, such as three-cueing, and more traditional phonics-based methods. In reality, the progressive methods usually dominate, with phonics usually thrown in as an afterthought, if at all.

She said that in her teacher education program there was no emphasis on phonics instruction and the key elements of the science of reading: "We weren't taught how to do that. How do I assess that? How do I track it? What methods do I use?" She received no instruction that would help her answer those crucial questions.

"I think there was more of an emphasis on how do you structure a lesson in general," she said, rather than being instructed on "what good reading pedagogy looks like."

After college she taught as a substitute teacher for two years, but because "it was super hard to get a job in Oregon at that time," she "just ended up in Colorado Springs, Colorado at a K-6 elementary school."

At her new small school, out of the four teachers, "Three of us were brand new teachers and there was one veteran on our team, who was so patient and sweet and just walked all three of us through our first year of teaching and our second year of teaching." "I think she retired after that," she laughed, "maybe we wore her out."

She also received teacher professional development instruction from a professor at the University of Colorado at Colorado Springs, "And, man, I just ate it up."

"It was so good," she said, "because I hadn't learned this stuff in college and she gave us more specific strategies."

For example, for the first time, she found out, "this is what phonics looks like and this is what a good comprehension lesson looks like."

Despite the assistance from her veteran colleague and the professional development, she realized, "I don't know how to teach reading."

"I remember the last kid going out on the last day of school, my first year teaching second grade, and the door shutting" she recalled, and "I was just like, I have to figure out how to teach kids to read."

"I know kids left my class, not where they needed to be," she said, "I vowed that I was never going to let that happen again."

Because she had initially taught sixth graders, "I didn't realize that I didn't know how to teach kids to read," but she realized her deficiency "being with the second graders who were at the beginning of their journey."

Motivated by the haunting thoughts of her underprepared students, "I actually started researching and digging around and asking other teachers and doing whatever it took to teach myself how to teach my students how to read."

She obtained a copy of the "Teaching Children to Read" report by the National Reading Panel, which underscored the importance of phonemic awareness, phonics, fluency, vocabulary, text comprehension, independent reading, and teacher professional development.[74]

She then studied the National Reading Panel's five essential components of reading discussed in detail at the beginning of

Chapter 4: phonemic awareness, phonics, vocabulary development, fluency, and comprehension.[75]

As she was focusing on how to become a more effective teacher of reading, she moved back to Oregon in 2012.

At her new school she said, "there are a lot of strugglers." While there are some students who have figured out how to read, "you have the ones that struggle, struggle, struggle."

For reference, Oregon, like in so many other states, has a lot of students who are not performing well in reading. On the 2022 National Assessment for Educational Progress eighth grade reading exam, nearly three-quarters—72 percent—of Oregon students taking the test failed to perform at the proficient level.[76]

Despite the large number of struggling readers, "at that point, I knew how to help them." And that meant that she was willing to go beyond the reading curriculum that the district supplied to her.

"I also knew that I didn't care what the curriculum the district gave me," she said, "I was going to find whatever the kids needed and use that."

The reading curriculum used then was "just balanced literacy," where "you're using the cues picked up from the pictures, and context, and maybe some memorization of as many words as you can to figure out what the words are on the page."

She also pointed to rules in the curriculum that do not always apply to the English language.

"So, it's trying to teach kids all these rules, but with all these exceptions, and everyone goes, 'Oh my gosh, English is crazy.'" For instance, she cited the example of "two vowels go walking and the first one does the talking."

This rule would apply to the word "boat," where two vowels are together, but only the first vowel—the letter "o"—is heard, i.e., "does the talking." However, in the word "create" both the letters "e" and the "a" are "talking," despite being next to each other.

Thus, she said that this rule "is only true 40 percent of the time," and "to teach kids something that's only true 40 percent of the time is crazy."

Under that curriculum, she said, there was no pattern or logic. And even when phonics showed up occasionally in the curriculum, it was not systematic.

In response to the deficiencies in her district's reading curriculum, she said that she supplemented it with lessons from *Reading Reflex* by Carmen and Geoffrey McGuiness, which emphasizes segmenting (separating sounds into words), blending (blending sounds into words), and phoneme manipulation (pulling sounds into and out of words).[77]

While balanced literacy is still the reading instruction model used at her school, she said, "I'm trying to shift my school to science of reading." Since most schools, like hers, still use balanced literacy curricula, "most teachers have not been trained in what is effective, so it's going to be a years-long process, and people need to get on board and be willing to give up what is not effective and move forward."

"I'm fighting that battle daily at my school," she said, "trying to help teachers understand, hey, you have to let go of doing this, the way you've always taught reading." "We have to do something different," she urged.

"Teachers realize the damage that is happening," she said, "and when they realize that what they're doing is not the best they would make a change."

"The district is saying that we paid all this money for this curriculum," she related, "you're going to use it." But, she smiled and said, "I really am a rebel."

With a note of defiance, she said, "I'll use [the curriculum] if it's what my students need and if it's effective, but if it's not then I'm not using it, because why would I do that?"

Insightfully, she observed, "It's always a battle between here's the curriculum, you need to use it, and use data to drive instruction," and, "I've never seen where both of them meet." In other words, data on what is effective has not impacted the type of curriculum chosen for use in her classroom.

She has told her district's superintendent, "I will be teaching science of reading and if that's not what you want me to do, then I don't want a job here." The superintendent has given her the freedom to operate, "so I'm like, alright, we're going to do science of reading." Teachers in her school are now getting training in science of reading, "so we are making some headway," but, "it just can't happen fast enough."

"We don't have to play this game," she said, but, rather, "we can teach teachers to be effective right from the get go and not have to fight with the curriculum and stuff."

She noted that we cannot lose sight of the fact that the real victims of poor reading instruction are children.

If a child "can't do reading, then you're going to struggle in all subjects." She pointed to the math textbook used in her school, which "reads like a novel, so if you're a struggling reader then I hate math because I can't access my workbook."

"Kids just feel terrible about themselves," she lamented, "they definitely feel it, they take it to heart for sure."

The situation at her school district is not isolated. She said it is a national problem.

She traces the problem to higher education teacher training programs: "I don't know of any teacher candidate programs at the university or college level that have started their candidates on the science of learning." Therefore, "we have years of whole language and balanced literacy [teachers] coming into schools ahead of us and that's nationwide."

For Bowers, there are three things that have to change: teacher candidate training, reading curricula, and teacher professional development. There must be a "paradigm shift and [we must] just get out of the old rut."

CHAPTER 6
Bad Reading Instruction Is Not Just in Public Schools

"My mother, back in the 1990s, was very much engaged in the reading wars, and she always firmly believed in phonics and the science of reading," recalled California parent Rebeka Sinclair.

"I was born in Pittsburgh, Pennsylvania and then went to Wisconsin when I was in the eighth grade," she said.

The oldest of four children, her father was an engineer and her mother was an accountant who decided to stay at home and raise the kids.

"It was an amazing childhood," she recalled, "with a lot of independence and freedom in suburbia in the Midwest."

Adding to her positive experience was the quality of her schooling. She attended public schools in Pennsylvania and Wisconsin. In Pennsylvania, "I was selected for the gifted and talented program and it was absolutely incredible." Her high school in Wisconsin was "a very highly ranked public school and I had a wonderful experience with athletics and teachers."

Because of her prowess in swimming, "I was recruited for swim teams in college" and although she did not know what the Ivy League meant, "I ended up going to Cornell University for my undergrad."

She said that attending regular public schools created a mindset in her when she went to Cornell: "I definitely came in with an underdog mentality, which was beneficial to me. There were a lot of students from very prestigious elite private schools and boarding schools [at Cornell]. And having that underdog mentality really gave me a leg up. I worked hard and it ended up not being as difficult as I thought it would be."

Having an analytical mind, she majored in economics and finance in college and "ended up having to go to work on Wall Street to pay off my student loans." She also had a passion for healthcare, so she became a healthcare finance professional.

After college, she moved to New York City, but eventually moved to California and eventually got married and had four children, becoming a stay-at-home mom.

She and her husband located to affluent Marin County, just north of the Golden Gate Bridge from San Francisco. They decided to send their children to an expensive private school, but would soon find out that a high tuition did not guarantee high quality instruction in reading.

The elite private schools in the area "would send teachers to Columbia Teachers College over the summer to attend the Lucy Calkins reading and writing workshop." At their children's school, "they would actually solicit donations from the parent community to send teachers to this program." Little did most parents know that they were funding the academic failure of their own children.

"We had no idea that this program de-emphasized phonics instruction," she said. "It was just off our radar."

"It was one of those situations," she said, "where all of the fancy private schools were using this curriculum, so it must have been the best, right?"

Lucy Calkins' program, however, was far from the best.

Education Week notes that Calkins' workshop-style curriculum emphasized teachers "demonstrate the skills and habits that good readers have, and then students practice them on their own in books of their choice, with teachers acting as guides."

However, the publication noted, "education researchers and curriculum evaluation organizations have argued that the materials don't explicitly teach the letter-sound knowledge that many kids need to learn how to read words—and they have argued that the curriculum's practice of matching kids with books at their purported 'level' can prevent equitable access to rich, complex text."[78]

Units of Study, Calkins' reading curriculum, received failing grades in the widely cited EdReports evaluation.

Reporting on EdReports' review of Calkins' curriculum, *Education Week* notes that, "the materials rely on cueing strategies for word identification: prompting students to draw on pictures, context, and sentence structure—along with letters—to figure out what words to say." However, "research has shown that pulling students' attention away from the letter can lower the chances that they'll be able to map the spelling to the spoken word in their memory."[79]

This evidence-based criticism of Calkins' theories resulted in the Teachers College at Columbia University eventually closing her Reading and Writing Project, which was housed at the school, in 2023.

With her two oldest children who went to that private school, Sinclair said she was lucky because they learned to read at a young age. "I would always talk to them about sounding out words and focusing a lot on phonics," she said, "and that is how we encouraged reading at home."

Her children's experience at school was very different.

"When my daughter was in kindergarten and first grade," she recalled, "they used a balanced literacy program," with "teachers teaching children how to use the cueing approach—instead of asking kids to sound out words they would focus on looking at clues to identify words." Describing the instruction, she explained:

Okay, we're stumbling on a word. What do the pictures teach us? What do you think this word means based on what you see? And the teachers would actually promote this methodology to parents. We weren't sounding out words. We were looking for clues to identify words. So really heavy focus on language comprehension reading a lot of different types of books, trying to figure it out on their own, with very little direct instruction on sounding out words and how does the English language work.

"So what we were taught from our progressive private school," she recounted, "was to ask the child to look for clues based on the sentence, maybe the beginning letter of the word, and the pictures." If the child was still struggling, "we would just tell them the word so they wouldn't get too upset."

"I saw a little bit of phonics," she said, but "they were not taught how to spell words, they were to figure it out on their own."

She emphasized, "So none of those strategies were the appropriate ones to take in terms of teaching a child to decode the written language."

It is often believed that only children from low-income backgrounds or from non-English-fluent families have reading issues. But in very affluent Marin County at this hugely expensive private school, the ineffective reading instruction caused many children to develop problems reading.

"So after paying an arm and a leg for tuition," she said, parents would be forced to pay for extra tutoring for their children. She said, "a lot of them would pay over $10,000 for a very intensive reading program over the summer."

"So they were spending so much money on the education of their children," she observed, "and they had to supplement to actually give their kids an appropriate reading curriculum." "It was so shocking to me," she said.

She remembered one wealthy couple—tech entrepreneurs married to each other—"and two out of their three kids at this fancy private school require $10,000 to $15,000 intensive reading programs because the private school is not able to teach their kids to read."

"In retrospect," she said, "it is wild."

It was not just in her private school in Marin County where the children had reading problems. Sinclair tells of a billionaire she knew in San Francisco whose children "went to these San Francisco private schools and they all required intensive reading support outside school."

Family affluence did not prevent children from having trouble reading. Rather, "when you think about the people that I knew who were paying for these supplementary programs, it's so indicative that it really points to the fact that the instruction was flawed."

Once again, the victims of this flawed instruction are the children.

She related a sad story: "Another friend at this private school, her poor child, when this instructional program didn't work, then the kid gets a label. Now they view her as having a processing disorder. Does that label stick with them for the rest of their life?"

"I think in these affluent schools, it's much easier to provide a label on a child," she said. While, "Possibly in the public schools that embraced these instructional methods, it's probably a lot easier to blame the parents—oh, there's not a lot of books at home or this child wasn't read to enough."

"It's much easier to point the finger than to really examine critically the way you're teaching and why you're teaching," she concluded.

After a few years in Marin County, Sinclair and her family moved to Orange County in Southern California and decided to send their children to public school.

Having learned her lesson in Northern California, "I definitely researched the elementary school to make sure it had phonics-based reading." It was fortunate that their neighborhood school did have a heavy emphasis on phonics because her third child, unlike her first two, had early reading issues.

"He is a different kid," she said, "and it definitely took longer for him to learn to read."

Thankfully, the school "had a tremendous early literacy intervention program with multiple specialists a the school to catch these kids [with reading problems]" and "it was 100-percent science of reading."

She observed, "It was so amazing, through this instruction, to really see reading click for him." Because the school used an effective reading instructional method, "we did not spend any money on extra tutors, and it clicked for him, and he's sounding out words and it's so cool to watch."

"I'm so thankful that our public school down here invested heavily in that," she said, "and compared to the private school in Marin County, it does seem to spend a lot of time on reading and phonics."

Interestingly, the private school in Marin County "seemed to spend more time on social justice topics, quite frankly." She said, "there was a very concerted effort to inject a lot of critical pedagogy and the social justice theme into the books the kids were getting."

Evidently, it was more important for the private school to indoctrinate than to educate kids on how to read well. "My husband and I definitely took issue with that."

In her son's public school, parents can choose reading selections, "so if I want my kids to be exposed to classical texts, they can read a classical text within this reading program at the public school."

In addition to "books that my kids can read at school, they can pick them at school, but if I wanted them to read a book at home they could read a book at home and then take a reading comprehension quiz." She said, "I can direct my kids away from a lot of the more recently published texts for kids that don't really do much to build a knowledge base, so that's something I really like."

Thus, if her son wanted to read J.R.R. Tolkien's classic tale *The Hobbit*, she would enter that title into a database, "and based on this database, they're given a reading comprehension quiz," which "makes sure that my child understood the book, tracks their reading level and the word count."

"I'm very thankful," she said, "that we can cultivate the literature selection because learning to read is half of it." "It's the acquisition of knowledge," she emphasized, "that should begin even in elementary school that can set the stage for them to contend for higher level ideas and science and history and social studies."

Her son now "loves to read, and we're working on more advanced books." Reading "is no longer a source of frustration, and I really attribute that to this targeted early intervention he got at the school."

She shudders to think how her son, who "has so much confidence now," would be like if he had "to go through an ineffective and inefficient reading program, he would really be struggling."

"I'm so happy that he has been set up for success by being taught this way," she said. She believes, "he has been given the right tools and he's right where he needs to be."

The phonics-based science-of-reading program has worked, not just for her son, but for the other children in the school. She said, "comparing the number of kids who needed this intensive reading intervention in the private-school community versus the public-school community down here, where they have different instructional methods and a lot of early intervention, it's a huge difference."

Looking at the bigger picture across the country, she observed, "It is so depressing to think that in a technologically advanced society that the true scientific method was so disregarded in such a foundational field for our children."

She is especially appalled at how ineffective progressive instructional methods came to dominate America's schools: "Teaching a child to read is the ultimate form of social justice, in my opinion, and the fact that these instructional methods were developed and celebrated without scientific scrutiny and then were able to be marketed and sold in a billion-dollar industry, again, without scientific rigor or accountability, it just shows you how broken the education system is in our country."

"This is what happens when you have a system that is not held accountable," she said. "There is no accountability in education and the system today perpetuates this type of injustice because there is no accountability."

Thank goodness, she noted, "for parents speaking up on this issue and asking questions, because to my knowledge, the questions started to come from parents of students getting diagnosed with dyslexia and that led to the media attention." Without parents questioning the failed reading model used so widely across the country, "who knows if this train would still be barreling down the track."

"It just shows," she said, "the institutional brokenness that can occur when debate is stifled, when no one questions narratives, or holds anyone accountable."

Going forward, she urged, "we need more accountability in our education system and we also need more parents to get very involved at the local level, analyzing curriculum as it's adopted by school boards, and not being afraid to ask questions and understanding the reason for making these purchases and the reason for teaching these foundational skills in this way."

CHAPTER 7
Fighting and Winning on the Local Level

"There has been this long simmering tension between parents and staff members—meaning teachers and administrators—over textbook selection," said California parent Sugi Sorensen.

Against huge odds, Sorensen and his fellow parents were able to overcome the intransigence, blocking tactics, and philosophical opposition of the school district, and force the district to jettison a balanced-literacy program in favor of "probably switching to structured literacy-based curriculum."

"I suspect that there's a tidal wave that's hitting the whole United States, and even in California, where school districts are wising up," he said.

He and his family live in the La Cañada-Flintridge area of Los Angeles County. He is a systems engineer for the world-famous Jet Propulsion Laboratory. His personal background story is detailed in greater length in Chapter 10, where his battles against failed mathematics curricula and instructional methods are described.

When it came to reading, he said that he had "read about the problems with our educational system," so "I needed to teach my kids the essential skills." He said that he "taught them how to read and tried to inculcate a passion for reading before they got to school because I didn't want to leave it to the school."

Because his children already had good reading skills when they entered public school, he did not become aware of the problems with the school's reading curriculum until he "was accepted to be on a curriculum review committee."

Having a seat on that committee, he was able to see that the various reading curriculum choices "were all balanced literacy in their approach."

He decided to do his own research, and "I started to find the issues with balanced literacy." After becoming aware of the problems with the balanced-literacy instructional approach, his reaction was, "Wow, this is messed up."

In California, before school districts adopt a curriculum, it is supposed to be piloted in certain classrooms to see if the curriculum actually improves the learning of students. He was appalled by the manner in which his district piloted the proposed curriculum.

"They were not systematic in their piloting," he said, "to measure before and after and have control groups." "I didn't know that they were this sloppy in their adoption process until I saw it on the committee for myself," he related.

How sloppy? In one of the schools piloting the proposed curriculum, "the teachers just flipped through the materials basically, and never taught a lesson."

So much for having evidence to support choosing a particular curriculum.

Overall, however, the district's administrators and teachers "were fully on board with balanced literacy."

Parents were mostly kept out of the curriculum-adoption process until the very end, and then they were only allowed at the vote-taking meeting as observers. He pointed out to the district that California's education code required parents to be involved in the selection process.

The district made it difficult for parents to even review proposed curricula. He recounted: "They gave you four hours on Friday to look through like six different vendors—products for seven grades. It was insane, like, how are you going to do that in four hours?"

After he complained to the district, viewing time was extended and "now the process is multiple weeks where you can go [and review]."

In addition to the balanced literacy reading curriculum, his district used Fountas & Pinnell's Benchmark Assessment System (BAS), which assessed student reading levels and reading comprehension levels for students. The district would use Fountas & Pinnell's leveled literacy intervention to address students' reading problems.

In an extensive report on BAS, American Public Media (APM) said it "is one of the most popular measures of early reading ability in American elementary schools." It is used "in about one in six American elementary schools." According to the report:

> The test attempts to identify children's reading abilities by judging how well they progress through a set of stories rated at increasingly difficult reading levels. Those "leveled books" are supposed to represent each point in the development of skilled reading, from Level A to Level Z.
>
> To administer the Benchmark Assessment System, a teacher has a child read a series of those books out loud. The process takes about 20 to 30 minutes for each student, and it can take even longer in the upper grades.[80]

He said that the leveled readers would "have pictures in them prominently displayed, and then they send the books home or the kids read them in class and they'll be assessed, which takes a long time."

The APM report found that the books used to score the BAS "use repetitive sentence patterns accompanied by illustrations that make guessing words easy so that a student can 'read' them even if they can't sound out the words in the sentence." Yet, "research dating back to the 1970s has shown that approach is ineffective and potentially harmful to children's progress in reading."[81]

Not only did the BAS take a long time to administer, it was inaccurate. Sorenson said that when his daughter was in the third grade, "she was reading middle-school-level books." However, "I noticed that in the Benchmark Assessment they're saying she's only reading 1.5 years above grade level, and I knew that was ridiculous."

At the time he did not question the BAS results for his daughter because he did not know all the faults with BAS. He eventually found a study by University of Florida education professor Matt Burns that found BAS was highly inaccurate. Further, he said, BAS "is even worse at identifying kids who had reading difficulty."

Burns, who conducted the first peer-reviewed study of BAS, told American Public Media "that until he decided to try, the test had never been independently validated to see how closely its results aligned with other assessments of early reading." What he found was shocking:

> One of his studies showed that the BAS was able to distinguish between proficient and struggling readers only about half the time; the odds were little better than chance.
>
> "So I could buy this test, train all my teachers to give it, take about 30 minutes per kid," Burns said. "Or really just have a teacher flip a coin for every kid, and they'll get it right just as often."
>
> And when it came to identifying the readers who were furthest behind, Burns said, the BAS performed even worse. It missed most of the struggling readers . . . It caught only 31%

of those students. Burns called that level of accuracy "shocking," saying it was "quite literally the lowest I've ever seen."

In that case, Burns said, "flipping a coin would actually be better."[82]

Fountas & Pinnell has released only a single study to support BAS, but APM pointed out that "even their own study casts doubt on reliability of the test." Only a little more than four out of 10 K-2 students reading two books at the same level scored at the same level on the assessment.[83]

Because it takes so long to administer, the BAS is very expensive. APM notes, "Fountas & Pinnell recommend getting a substitute [teacher] to fill for one or two days, so the teacher has enough time to get through the entire class."[84]

Yet, "Burns has found that other tests, which are available online for free and take as little as three minutes to administer, were more accurate than the BAS, which can cost close to $500 per classroom and is far more time-consuming."[85]

Other research has found, "The BAS took so long to administer that, accounting for staff time, it cost double or triple what the other tests did," with the recommendation "against using it to identify struggling readers."[86]

For all its high expense, the big question is why is the BAS such a poor predictor of student reading ability? Burns believes that the leveled books do not accurately measure the ability of students to read:

> In another study, Burns asked second and third graders to read aloud from two books, both at their designated level. As the children read, he took a simple measure of the number of words they read correctly per minute. He said he expected the scores to match up closely. But just as Fountas and Pinnell noted in their own study almost a decade earlier, he found that

students' reading of the two books was, at best, only moderately correlated.

"There's not a lot of consistency," Burns explained. "They read those two books with a very different level of skill. That means there's something else other than the supposed reading level contributing to how well they read these books." He inferred that a child's vocabulary and background knowledge about a topic matter far more. A kid who's obsessed with sharks, for instance, might be able to read a story set in an aquarium well above their expected reading level.

Likewise, it can be difficult for a test to distinguish between a student struggling to read words and one struggling to understand an unfamiliar subject with all its new vocabulary. It would be like asking a literature professor to summarize a car repair manual; it probably wouldn't indicate much about their overall reading ability.[87]

Unfortunately, Sorensen said, "I think most parents are like me and they only pay attention when there's a problem" and "they use report cards as an indication of whether there's a problem." So, "if things are going fine, parents really don't care."

But what if the assessment is telling parents that their children are doing fine, but they really are not?

The APM report spotlighted a San Francisco mom whose son in Kindergarten could not recognize letters by sight or write them. Yet, the BAS said that her son was reading at a level appropriate for his age.[88]

By the end of her son's year in first grade, this mother badgered the school district to give her son a more comprehensive reading evaluation, which "showed her son was so far behind his peers in reading and writing that he fit the profile for dyslexia."[89]

"The Benchmark Assessment System," reported APM, "had been—and would continue to be—wrong about how well he could read."[90]

Sadly, this mom's son, who is now in the seventh grade, still struggles with reading. The San Francisco school superintendent admits that a student can succeed on BAS but still not be literate.[91] That shocking admission means that his school district and so many others across America have failed the nation's children.

Sorensen related a similar experience from parents he knew through their common membership in a group concerned about Fountas & Pinnell.

Parents would tell teachers that their children had reading problems, but teachers would pooh-pooh their concerns and say that parents should just read to their children and that children would figure out reading.

However, Sorensen said, "what usually wound up happening, at least for this parent group, is eventually they would get a diagnosis and they would get reading intervention." But since the quality of the school's reading intervention program "was mediocre at best," the parents all went to "outside tutors to address the issue that they observed with their kids."

A number of these parents decided to use Orton-Gillingham-certified tutors. As previously discussed, Orton-Gillingham is a multi-sensory phonics-based remedial reading instruction technique. He said, "later they got this type of specific intervention from the tutors, they saw much more improvement than they were seeing using what the school was prescribing."

In his district, "I learned later that the parents of dyslexic kids had banded together and demanded that they change the curriculum." These parents had to remediate their children, "so they had started complaining to the district."

"They had gone to battle with the district," he recalled, "and said what you're using is insufficient and not helping our kids enough." These parents achieved a partial victory when the district compromised and instituted an intervention for dyslexia curriculum that was somewhat better.

Parents' use of outside tutors and parent pressure to change ineffective curriculum masks the incompetence of schools and districts. He said that his children's school district was high performing, "in spite of what they teach in schools, not because of what they teach."

"Schools never bother to take systematic surveys of how much supplementation and tutoring is going on," so "they don't know." Thus, "they're sending false signals."

He minces no words, saying that "this bad curriculum caused all these parents to go supplement outside," caused the high test scores. "But it has nothing to do with the curriculum," he pointed out, "it's the compensation and reaction from parents."

Momentum, though, was on the side of the parents in Sorensen's district.

One of the district's top administrators was on the side of parents and the science of reading. She had reviewed how reading was taught in the district and she concluded, according to Sorensen, that it was "sort of a balkanized patchwork, it's ad hoc, and that's not acceptable."

She then said that she wanted "all our teachers trained on science of reading" and "all the teachers came along."

Even more amazing and heartening, he said, "now they're at the point where they decided they're getting rid of Fountas and Pinnell Benchmark Assessment System next year." And with textbook adoption in the district coming up "in the next two years, they'll probably switch to the structured literacy-based curriculum."

Even now, he said, "I'm hearing anecdotally from parents and some of my parent groups that they're already seeing changes in the classroom." According to one parent of a kindergartner with whom he spoke, "these changes are already occurring, there's more emphasis on phonics, and my kid is reading better."

Change for the better, therefore, is possible, even in California.

CHAPTER 8
A California Legislator With a Plan

"For me," observed California State Assemblymember Blanca Rubio, "the science of reading provides the non-judgmental part of teaching; you're not judging kids; you're delivering instructions based on data."

A former elementary school teacher who taught low-income Black, Latino, and White children in the industrial city of Fontana in California's Inland Empire, Rubio said that with reading instruction based on the science of reading "we're giving them the foundation that they need to be successful, regardless of color."

A current four-term member of the California State Assembly, she was elected as a Democrat to represent a diverse district in Southern California. Her life story underscores the importance of giving children the right learning tools to succeed.

Born in Mexico, she is the oldest of five siblings, one of whom is her sister Susan who serves as a California state senator.

As a small child in a school in Mexico, she recalled being taught letter sounds, such as the double r's used in Spanish. "I remember that it was phonemic awareness," she said.

After moving back and forth from the U.S. to Mexico, her family eventually came to California.

In school in Los Angeles, Blanca and Susan knew some English but their brother did not so he was misdiagnosed with a learning disability.

"The issue was language barrier," said Rubio, but by the time the school district "figured out he was misdiagnosed or misplaced in the classroom, it was already three years later, so it was too late." Sadly, "He dropped out of high school in the ninth grade."

She faced her own challenges, even though she said, "I'm the oldest and I knew I was smart." When she went to her high school counselor to get guidance about attending college, the counselor said: "Oh, honey, you're just going to get pregnant—literally told me that," and "there was no path for me in college."

Despite such shocking obstacles, she said, "I was the first one to try and kick down doors." She eventually attended East Los Angeles College and then transferred to Azusa Pacific College, where she received her bachelor's degree in business.

She ended up going into teaching and spent 16 years in the classroom. During her teaching career she focused on using data to guide her instructional practices. As she said, "I know that math does not lie and anything that has to do with data and numbers, I'm kind of a geek."

Because of her view that "data is king in teaching," she gravitated to the science of reading.

"We need teachers to be deliberate in the instruction," she said, "not hoping and praying that it'll work." She admonished, "hope and pray is not a strategy."

Convinced by the data supporting the effectiveness of the science of reading she decided to introduce legislation in 2024, AB 2222, which would integrate the core tenets of the science of reading in accreditation policies, teacher training, and curriculum decisions.[92]

The text of her bill first declares the disturbing reading landscape in California: only "3 in 10 third grade pupils from low-income families are on grade level in English language arts," while among "low-income Black pupils, English learners, and pupils with disabilities, the gaps widen with only 2 in 10 pupils in each respective group on grade level in English language arts in third grade."[93]

In addition to these statistics from California's state reading test, results on the 2022 National Assessment of Educational Progress show that only 13 percent of Black fourth graders, 21 percent of Hispanic fourth graders, and 21 percent of low-income fourth graders in California score at or above the proficient level in reading.[94]

Not surprisingly, the bill text proclaims, "California has one of the lowest adult literacy rates in the nation," which results in adults being "more at risk for remaining in poverty, less likely to be employable, more socially isolated, and less likely to live healthy lives."[95]

Her bill estimates that eradicating illiteracy in California would increase the state's gross domestic product by $360 billion.[96]

Citing decades of research that "demonstrate strong evidence about how pupils develop literacy skills," her bill states: "Oral language development, in combination with evidence-based literacy instruction grounded in the elements of the science of reading—explicit and systematic instruction in phonological and phonemic awareness, phonics, vocabulary, fluency, comprehension, and writing—has clearly proven benefits for pupils, including English learners."[97]

Therefore, "California must take bolder measures to address inequities and create a clear, comprehensive, and evidence-based approach for ensuring that all pupils are proficient, skilled readers by the end of elementary school and that they are equipped to succeed in middle school, high school, and beyond."[98]

Specifically, "Those measures include enacting policies that will ensure all classroom instructional materials used to teach children to read will be grounded in the science of reading, and that all current and future teachers will be trained in the science of reading."[99]

The bill then spells out how the science of reading must be incorporated into teacher credentialing policies, accreditation processes for teacher training programs, professional development programs for teachers, and instructional materials.[100]

The bill prohibits districts from adopting non-science-of-reading instructional materials unless granted a waiver by the state board of education.[101]

A key provision of the bill recognizes the importance of changing the direction of teacher training programs in the California State University and University of California systems. The bill seeks to provide "professional development aligned with the science of reading to faculty members who teach literacy and reading instruction at accredited institutions with approved educator preparation programs."[102]

The state's teacher training programs are in desperate need of realignment. The National Council on Teacher Quality graded 41 teacher preparation programs in California based on "attention to the five core components of scientifically based reading instruction—phonemic awareness, phonics, fluency, vocabulary, and comprehension."[103]

The review deducted points if the programs promoted content that was "contrary to research-based practices," such as balanced literacy.[104]

Shockingly, 31 out of the 41 teacher prep programs in California received a D or F grade. Among the programs receiving an F grade were well known universities such as California Polytechnic State University-San Luis Obispo, San Diego State University, and San Jose State University, none of which covered even a single component of the science of reading adequately.[105]

Overall, concluded the NCTQ review, "California ranks among the worst in the nation for the average number of components of reading its program adequately address."[106]

The state of reading ability in California is so poor that Rubio's bill has drawn support of legislators from diametrically opposite sides of the ideological spectrum, from her fellow Democrat Assemblymember Corey Jackson, best known for advocating for reparations for African Americans, to Assembly Republican leader James Gallagher.

"Let's put everything aside," she said, "and let's focus on what the outcomes for our children are going to be."

"What they do have in common," she said, "is they care about kids." On this issue, "They don't care about their political ideology, they're caring about the outcomes for kids."

Indeed, a broad array of groups are supporting her bill, including the state NAACP, the state PTA, and Decoding Dyslexia California.

"We must prioritize equitable access to opportunity for children by ensuring they can read," said state NAACP president Rick Callender. "This is not just an education issue, it is a social justice issue."[107]

There are, however, pockets of opposition to her bill.

The California Teachers Association, the state's largest teachers union, opposes the bill claiming, "Educators are best equipped to make school and classroom decisions to ensure student success."[108] Yet, that statement flies in the face of the state's rock-bottom student reading scores. If teachers were making the best decisions about ways to teach reading to students then California's reading proficiency rates would be much higher.

The NCTQ's finding that the large majority of California's teacher training programs receive D or F grades for teaching prospective teachers about effective science-of-reading instructional methods reveals the hollowness of the CTA's claim.

Marshall Tuck, head of the education reform organization EdVoice, which supports her bill, responded to the CTA's opposition saying, "Unfortunately, a lot of folks in the field haven't actually been trained on [the science of reading], and a lot of the instruction materials in classrooms today don't align with that."[109]

In addition to the CTA, the California Association of Bilingual Educators (CABE) opposes the bill. Rubio said that she had a virtual meeting with CABE leaders who argued that her bill was a "one size fits all" response to the learning problems faced by English language learners.

It is important to note that research shows that English language learners (ELLs) benefit from components of the science of reading, such as phonemic awareness and phonics. A comprehensive study by the University of Alabama found: "For ELLs, phonological awareness should have an increased emphasis alongside phonics instruction. English learners benefit from explicit instruction on the phoneme differences between their first and second languages and parallel morphological awareness instruction."[110]

The study found, "Early intervention in phonology and morphology alongside phonics are beneficial for this ELL student subgroup."[111]

Recall that phonology involves the sound structures of spoken words and phonemic awareness is central to phonology. Morphology involves morphemes, which are the smallest unit of meaning in a language (e.g., the "s" morpheme of nouns in the plural form).

Rubio, who had been a member of CABE when she was teaching, pressed the group's leaders for specific reasons for their opposition. She invited them to come to Sacramento, at her expense, to go over her bill line by line so "you can help me craft a bill that is acceptable to you." "Their answer," she said ruefully was, "Assemblymember, it's just philosophical differences."

Her response? "I hung up," she exclaimed, "because then our conversation is not being constructive."

"Give me the data or give me the solutions to what you think the problem is," she said.

"But not engaging at all," she said, is wrong because "you have to be able to provide solutions"

She knew then, "that's when it became political, because it wasn't the policy." If it was policy, "they would have sat with me and said, 'Okay, this we can live with, this we can live with, and let's figure it out."

"But just to oppose [the bill] just on philosophical differences is B.S.," she emphasized.

"We're not building cars," she observed, "we are creating kids, lifelong learners, and we want kids to be able to learn and to be successful."

Unfortunately, too often, "The kids are suffering from political ideology."

Yet, those pushing political ideology over kids, such as the teachers union, have clout. State Assembly leaders shelved Rubio's bill for 2024 without a hearing. Her bill can be re-introduced in 2025.[112]

"If we don't look beyond the political B.S.," she warned, "and look at the outcomes then we're absolutely having the wrong conversations."

SECTION THREE: THE COLLAPSE OF MATH SKILLS

CHAPTER 9
Why Is Math Achievement Falling and What Can Be Done About It?

With student math proficiency at historic lows, it is easy to forget that national math scores were actually rising in the early 2000s.

A 2020 study by the Massachusetts-based Pioneer Institute found that U.S. students "had made slow but relatively steady improvement in mathematics achievement," with scores modestly increasing on the eighth-grade National Assessment of Educational Progress math exam "every two years from 2003 until 2013."[113]

However, from 2013 to 2019, the year before the COVID-19 pandemic, average eighth-grade NAEP math scores "have generally declined and remain at a level that is statistically significantly lower" than before 2013.[114]

What happened in the early 2010s that could have caused this reversal of student math performance?

Answer: the controversial Common Core national education standards were implemented in most states during that time period.

Common Core is a set of subject-matter standards that became de-facto national standards after the Obama administration used billions of dollars in federal funding to entice states to replace their own state standards with Common Core. Testing and classroom curricula are now aligned to the Common Core national standards.

What is especially troubling about Common Core, according to the Pioneer Institute study, is that struggling students were the ones who were most affected by its negative impacts on math skills:

> Grade 8 math achievement for students at the 75th percentile, which was improving gradually before Common Core, has plateaued and remained at about the same level . . . Students who were average (50th percentile) or below before Common Core have declined since its implementation, with the steepest declines experienced by students at the 25th and 10th percentiles, those already the furthest behind.[115]

The study also examined the impact of Common Core on student math performance on the ACT college entrance exam. While acknowledging that students self-select to take the exam, the study still said that it was illustrative in each year from 2013 to 2019, "we see a sustained decline since the implementation of Common Core."[116]

Other studies have also found that Common Core has adversely impacted student math performance.

A large-scale 2019 study put out by the federally funded Center for Standards, Alignment, Instruction, and Learning (C-SAIL) examined NAEP test scores from 2010 to 2017. The study's authors had assumed that Common Core would raise student performance, but, instead, they found that Common Core "had a significant negative effect on the 8th graders' math achievement 7 years after adoption based on analyses of NAEP composite scores."[117]

Student performance declined significantly in specific areas, such as numbers properties, the longer Common Core was in effect.[118]

Further, Mengli Song, one of the co-authors of the study, noted, "When we examined NAEP scores by key student subgroups, we found larger and more significant negative effects for certain subgroups, particularly students with disabilities, English learners and Hispanic students, than we saw overall."[119]

"Going into the study, we certainly expected to discover some positive impacts — at least small ones," said Song, but "that is not what we found."[120]

Song told the education publication *Chalkbeat*: "It's rather unexpected. The magnitude of the negative effects [of Common Core] tend to increase over time."[121]

In view of this decline in math test scores, the question then becomes why has Common Core negatively impacted student math outcomes?

There are two ways to answer this question. The first is to look into the weeds and explore the type of math teaching methods that Common Core promotes. Second, one needs to take a step back and examine the structure of Common Core, especially including the level of student math knowledge that it recommends for each grade level.

A detailed review of Common Core math standards authored by Common Core expert Erin Tuttle and J.R. Wilson, co-author of the highly praised book *Traditional Math*, for the American Principles Project, found major instructional deficiencies across a variety of teaching areas.[122]

One of the key foundational tools of mathematics is the so-called "standard algorithm." According to Tuttle and Wilson:

> A mathematical algorithm is an ordered sequence of steps followed guaranteed to solve a specific class of math problems. An example of a class of problems would be adding numbers with any number of digits together or multiplying two numbers. To be considered an al-

gorithm, the steps must always provide a correct answer for all problems in that class. A standard algorithm is the most efficient and universally practiced algorithm for a particular class.[123]

Common Core does acknowledge and includes the standard algorithm and in a fourth-grade standard on addition gives the following example:[124]

$$\begin{array}{r} {\overset{1\ 1}{}} \\ 6\,7\,3 \\ +\,4\,5\,7 \\ \hline 1\,1\,3\,0 \end{array}$$

Most people recognize the standard algorithm for addition since it forms the foundation of their knowledge of how to add numbers. However, while Common Core includes the standard algorithm for addition, it does so in the fourth grade, much later than is usually the case.

Instead of having students learn the standard algorithm for addition in the earlier grades, Tuttle and Wilson note that the K-3 standards require students to solve addition and subtraction by, for example:

> . . . making ten (e.g., 8 + 6 = 8 + 2 + 4 = 10 + 4 = 14); decomposing a number leading to a ten (e.g., 13 - 4 = 13 - 3 - 1 = 10 - 1 = 9); and by creating equivalent but easier or known sums (e.g., adding 6 + 7 by creating the known equivalent 6 + 6 + 1 = 12 + 1 = 13)." These strategies are required *before* students are taught the standard algorithms in 4th grade.[125]

Also, instead of students simply learning the standard algorithm for subtraction in the first grade, Common Core says that students should use their fingers to subtract one number from another. Yet, say Tuttle and Wilson, Common Core "fails to offer or require the standard algorithm to be taught alongside it."[126] The emphasis is on understanding the concept rather than learning the procedure. Thus, students do not learn the standard algorithm for subtraction until the fourth grade.

Also, instead of having students memorize their multiplication tables, a Common Core document says that 8 x 3 can be solved by counting by threes: "The number of 3s is tracked with fingers or a visual or a physical (e.g., head bobs) pattern. For 8 x 3, you know the number of 3s and count by 3 until you reach 8 of them."[127] Imagine all the extra time and work this method requires versus just committing math facts and operations to memory and being able to automatically recall them.

Children are also asked to use other indirect methods such as drawing pictures. In the fourth grade, students are asked to multiply numbers by illustrating using rectangular arrays and/or area models. The standard multiplication algorithm is not taught until the fifth grade.[128]

Unfortunately, as Tuttle and Wilson point out, "There is also a risk (or probability) that students will not master and automatically use the standard algorithms, which are the quickest, most efficient methods that work in every situation." Therefore, "Students may form a habit of using less efficient, cumbersome strategies and methods that are taught or self-formulated which do not always produce correct answers, causing an over-reliance on calculators."[129]

Indeed, Common Core delays student use and understanding of all the foundational standard algorithms, which has serious consequences for students as they confront more difficult math subjects.

Tuttle and Wilson state: "The development and delay of the standard algorithms for the basic math operations of addition, subtraction, multiplication, and division contribute to an inadequate preparation for algebra." Specifically, they observe:

> The standard algorithm for long division is considered an essential tool for success in al-

gebra, yet [Common Core math standards] do not require fluency with it until the end of 6th grade. This delay leaves an inadequate amount of time for mastery if pre-algebra is to begin in 7th grade, which is necessary to reach Algebra I by the beginning of 8th grade. It also reduces the available time to master it and explore the nuance of different types of examples, such as divide by zero, or fractional division.[130]

The importance of reaching algebra in the eighth grade is crucially important, they say:

Preparation for a full Algebra I course by the beginning of 8th grade is critical for students who wish to reach Calculus in high school. Without completing Algebra I in 8th grade, students must take five years of math in four years. This is a doable feat for adept and motivated students, but one most students will choose to avoid. To increase the number of students reaching Calculus in high school, K-7 math standards should be structured to prepare all students for Algebra I. That will place more students on that path.[131]

However, because Common Core does not adequately prepare students to tackle algebra by the eighth grade, it pushes the teaching of algebra to the ninth grade, which brings one to a key structural problem with Common Core.

Delaying algebra until the ninth grade means that students will not be able to reach calculus by twelfth grade unless they compress five years of math subjects (algebra 1, geometry, algebra 2, pre-calculus, and calculus) into four years—an impossible ask for most students.

Also, pushing algebra to the ninth grade is not keeping in line with the practice in high-performing math countries in

East Asia, despite Common Core's claim to be comparable to top international standards.

In an article for the Hoover Institution at Stanford University, former U.S. assistant secretary of education Williamson Evers and former U.S. Department of Education senior policy advisor Ze'ev Wurman noted, "Children in Singapore and South Korea, for example, master introductory algebra in eighth grade or earlier," yet, Common Core "pushed the Algebra 1 course firmly into high school."[132]

Pre-Common Core efforts to increase the number of students taking algebra in the eighth grade had been hugely successful.

In California, the state's pre-Common Core math standards, which were adopted in 1997, were designed to prepare students for algebra in the eighth grade. As a result, the percentage of students taking eighth-grade algebra skyrocketed.

According to Evers and Wurman, "While in 1999 only 16 percent of students took algebra in eighth grade, four times as many, or 67 percent, took it in 2013 by eighth grade." Crucially, the success rate of these students also increased:

> This huge increase did not lower the success rate. In fact, the success rates of those students kept rising even as their enrollment exploded. To give a better sense of this growth, the number of successful early-algebra-takers rose from about 52,000 in 2002 to about 170,000 in 2013, while the cohort size barely budged.[133]

Further, "Fifty-five percent of California's eighth-grade test takers tested 'proficient' or 'advanced' on the California Standards Test in 2013, up from just under 40 percent in 2002."[134]

Preparing students for algebra in eighth grade and giving them the chance to do so "gave them the opportunity to make it to pre-calculus and calculus in high school, which would prepare them for selective colleges and STEM."[135]

Evers and Wurman point out that one particular benefit of pushing all students to take algebra in eighth grade was the impact on minority students, with the success rates increasing "by factors of five for African Americans and six for Latinos and [low-income] students." They observed, "California had made remarkable progress in narrowing the achievement gap—a goal often talked about, but rarely accomplished."[136]

However, when California implemented Common Core in 2014-15, all that progress came to a screeching halt. By 2017, Evers and Wurman lamented, "the number of eighth graders taking Algebra 1 in California dropped precipitously to 19 percent," which was "back to where it was around 1999, when early algebra taking was the privilege of the elite."[137]

Tragically, "while all demographic groups lost ground, the loss for Latino and African-American students was much deeper than for white and Asian Americans."[138]

Evers and Wurman conclude:

> Common Core proponents repeatedly praise it for its "rigor," how it will prepare children for the twenty-first century, enable more American students to pursue STEM, and increase America's competitiveness in the world. Yet when it comes to the clearest benchmark of rigor and expectations on par with international high-achievers—Algebra I in eighth grade—the Common Core not only punted, but it retarded and reversed the progress California had made during the pre-Common Core period, and the Common Core regress disproportionally hit disadvantaged minorities. The reduced rigor in K-8 education has resulted in less enrollment in advanced mathematics courses in high school, particularly of low-income and minority students. This reduces their chances of pursuing challenging and rewarding careers . . . .[139]

While the education establishment dutifully carried out Common Core's dictate to delay algebra until the ninth grade, parents have revolted against the Common Core status quo.

In San Francisco in 2023, parents sued the city's school district. As the *San Francisco Chronicle* reported, these parents demanded "officials put Algebra 1 back into middle schools for those ready to take it and stop forcing students to re-take the course in ninth grade if they have already passed it in private school or through other providers prior to entering high school."[140]

The San Francisco school district had a policy of not offering algebra in eighth grade, but rather requiring students to take algebra in ninth grade.

The parents' lawsuit contended that the district's policies "hobble children whose academic growth in mathematics out-paces that of their peers, create barriers which prevent students from excelling in mathematics, and make it nearly impossible for any student to attain access to high school calculus."[141]

A top district official acknowledged, "We do have a social justice agenda." The district believed that delaying algebra for all children until the ninth grade would increase the number of African-American and Hispanic students taking higher-level math courses.[142]

However, according to a study by researchers at Stanford University, "A controversial equity-focused mathematics reform in San Francisco Unified School District (SFUSD) featured de-laying Algebra I until ninth grade for all students." This policy did not achieve its equity goal: "Large ethnoracial gaps in ad-vanced math course-taking remained."[143]

The district's failure did not surprise parents. San Francisco parent leader Patrick Wolff said, "SFUSD has done a terrible job of teaching kids math." Children "who are capable of learn-ing more math have been held back for no good reason and kids who need more support in order to reach their full potential have absolutely been failed in receiving the support and instruc-tion they need."[144]

In the face of the research evidence, the parents' lawsuit, and a ballot initiative aimed at restoring eighth-grade algebra, the district caved. It agreed to start piloting opportunities for students to take algebra in the eighth grade in fall 2024 and open up a pathway for algebra to return to all middle schools by 2026-27.

The district revealed its new policy weeks before the public vote on the ballot initiative. The measure ended up winning in a crushing landslide.

Wolff observed: "The voters have made it very clear they want our public schools to teach as many kids as much as possible. The people of San Francisco understand that true equity and justice in our public schools never requires compromising academic excellence."[145]

If Common Core and the practices it promotes are counterproductive for student math learning, then what methods are better?

Similar to the evidence-based science of reading, there is now a movement called the Science of Math that uses "objective evidence about how students learn math in order to make educational decisions and to inform policy and practice." Proponents of the Science of Math "rely on well-researched instructional approaches and research about how students learn."[146]

Specifically, to help students achieve math proficiency, the Science of Math recommends that teachers should:

- Use a focused, coherent progression of math learning with emphasis on proficiency in key topics.
- Develop conceptual understanding, procedural fluency, and problem-solving skills at the same time.
- Use multiple approaches to meet the needs of students; explicit instruction should be used regularly.
- Focus on proficiency with whole numbers, fractions, geometry, and measurement; these are critical for algebra.
- Use formative assessment on a regular basis to assess student learning.[147]

Explicit instruction, which is "unambiguous, structured, systematic, and scaffolded instruction," is critically important. Scaffolded instruction involves breaking up learning into manageable chunks for students. Explicit instruction has three major parts: modeling, practice, and support.[148]

Modeling means "a step-by-step explanation on how to work a math problem." Practice includes "guided practice—this is where the teacher and students work on the same problems together," plus independent practice by the student himself or herself. Support involves the teacher asking students questions to check for understanding and, "Providing affirmative feedback for correct responses and corrective feedback for misconceptions."

Rather than have students discover math knowledge largely on their own, as many progressives prefer, the Science of Math states: "Explicit instruction offers value through sequencing of tasks in increments of difficulty, fluency building that promotes effective practice, and scaffolded opportunities for students to combine learned skills with new knowledge."[149]

Further, as opposed to progressive theories that push conceptual understanding first and then procedural knowledge, the Science of Math says that conceptual understanding and procedural knowledge support each other and should be taught together.[150]

Progressive educators claim that focusing on simply getting the correct answer causes rote learning of math procedures such as an algorithm, which is "a step-by-step procedure for solving a problem." Instead, these progressive educators "believe that struggling or grappling with challenging math tasks causes students to gain a deeper understanding than would be achieved if they learned the same skill without a struggle." Yet, according to the Science of Math, the reality is that forcing students to struggle is counterproductive:

> Productive struggle does not deepen understanding, grit, or creative problem solving. Productive struggle can lead to frustration and cause students

to develop misconceptions. In addition, the 'false starts' involved in struggle with challenging tasks without adequate support or guidance lead to lost instructional time and inefficiency.

No evidence suggests giving students partial information for making connections leads to learning. The idea comes from constructivism, which runs counter to what we understand about math learning. Students learning new skills require clear demonstrations and guided practice with immediate feedback. New concepts are not learned by struggling. Making connections relies on a foundation of learned knowledge.[151]

Finally, many progressive educators believe that timed tests cause math anxiety among students. Yet, the Science of Math notes, "No studies have determined that timed tests cause math anxiety—defined as feelings of apprehension, tension, or fear that may interfere with performance on math-related tasks." Rather, "timed tactics improve math performance":

- Timed tests provide critical information for student mastery of key skills and concepts.
- Timed tasks are fluency-building activities.
- Timed activities are necessary to promote math mastery when students have established a high level of accuracy and conceptual understanding.
- Fluency is a necessary dimension of math mastery associated with robust understanding and flexible problem solving.[152]

All the issues highlighted in this chapter regarding ineffective versus effective math instruction are discussed in greater detail by the parents and math instructors profiled in the ensuing chapters of this section.

CHAPTER 10
Parent and JPL Systems Engineer Fights for More Effective Math Instruction

"I think you'll find with other people like myself, it's always the same thing," observed Sugi Sorensen. "It's when your kids get to school and then you realize how deficient education is at school."

When it comes to understanding the deficiencies of math education, however, Sorensen is no ordinary parent.

A longtime systems engineer at the world-renowned Jet Propulsion Laboratory, he explained, "I'm an operations engineer and manage a process and a large custom-built software system that schedules the giant antennas that talk to spacecraft."

Whether the space missions are American, European, or Japanese, "then you need to use our Deep Space Network, which are these very large antennas that are stationed in specific locations around the world" and "we manage around 20 antennas around the [globe]."

The son of an American father of Danish and British extraction and a mother who emigrated from Japan to the United

States, he was born in Orange County in Southern California and attended public schools there. He eventually graduated from Harvey Mudd College with a degree in engineering.

Of his high school he said, "I thought it was a good school until I got to college and then I realized how horribly deficient my public schooling had been compared to all my peers."

"I hadn't taken calculus in high school," he recalled, yet "all my classmates had except one."

Likewise, "I thought I was a good writer and then my freshman rhetoric class disabused me of that delusion."

Even where he held his own, such as in social studies, "a lot of that was from outside reading, it wasn't from my school."

Looking back, he reflected, "I think one of the big problems of school is that parents just think it's a binary decision: 'Oh I'm going to pick where my kid goes to school and then I'm not going to worry about it.'"

"That was my parents," he said.

After college, he asked his father why he did not pay more attention in picking a school for him. His dad replied that he simply thought that moving to a nicer neighborhood would guarantee a good school—a mistake that many middle-class Americans make and which they do not realize until it is often too late for their children.[153]

Given his own personal education history, he originally did not want his children to attend public school. However, the family budget at the time would not allow for that option, so he and his wife eventually sent their children to public school in the La Cañada Unified School District in Los Angeles County.

He had started to teach his children reading and math when they were very young, "so by the time they got into kindergarten they were already a couple years ahead."

Initially, because his children were so far ahead, "I didn't really pay close attention to their math assignments because they could already do them and they never had any homework because they could finish it in class."

However, because his children were advanced, he then ran into the first sign of "one size fits all" rules.

He and other parents asked if their advanced children could do more advanced math during math time, but the school said, "no, they have to do what everyone else does."

On back-to-school days, he would talk to his child's teacher and ask if it was possible for his child to receive advanced math instruction: "Please excuse them from being bored and let them work on something else, and every year it was 'no.'" Even worse, "They would do things like give them Sudoku puzzles to do."

"So they're stuck in a one size fits all," he lamented.

Ironically, the equity ideology that wants to force equal math results for all children ends up fostering an inequitable reality.

"There's this whole shadow system we have of math learning centers in our district," he observed. In more affluent neighborhoods, "where there's a demand and parents are able to pay, the free market responds by providing these opportunities, but I'm helping friends that are in other districts that are not socio-economically advantaged and they don't have these options so it's a very inequitable situation."

In other words, equity begets inequity.

Also, public schools, like other government entities, value control. He got a taste of the school's determination to control instruction when he introduced a program called Math Olympiad. The program offers math competitions throughout the school year and starts in fourth grade.

Initially, the school was fine with the program and he said it became wildly popular among students, with up to a third of the school's students in a grade taking Math Olympiad.

"I would go teach once a week to fourth, fifth, and sixth graders," he said, and "I would get multiple other parents who were STEM professionals to come teach, so we were teaching three sessions a week."

"So that was an opportunity," he pointed out, "for those of us who were instructors to teach the kids advanced math like introducing them to algebra when they're in elementary school."

"We were meeting the demand by volunteering our services and the school didn't have to do anything," he said. "We built this whole math culture."

He said, "We were offering robotics classes, coding classes, all sorts of things."

But as so often happens in public education, no good deed goes unpunished.

"The district went from being supportive to being confrontational," he recounted, "and they eventually took the Math Olympiad program over from parents that were teaching it and now they have teachers teaching it and it's died in its popularity, so it's probably half the enrollment it used to be."

Eventually, he said, "they didn't like it" and "they said that it's inequitable, even though I always made it open to everybody." Further, "I think they just got fed up with parents creating this whole system."

"They're so obsessed with egalitarianism," he observed, "and so I would say what you should do is allow your teachers to innovate and offer different choices and allow your schools to compete against each other, and that just horrified them and they said we can't do that."

The school's takeover of the Math Olympiad paled in comparison to the district's decision to adopt the *Everyday Math* curriculum.

"Most parents don't pay attention to curriculum adoption," he said, "so I think somebody actually told me about it and when we started to look into it we found just this nightmare of a track record of *Everyday Math* everywhere."

Indeed, the critics of *Everyday Math* are legion.

For example, writing in the publication *City Journal*, Matthew Clavel, a teacher in New York City, observed that *Everyday Math* emphasized "'critical thinking skills' over old-fashioned drilling and the mastery of facts," so that what matters "is showing that you understand a concept, not whether you can perform a calculation and come up with a right answer."[154]

Yet, Clavel noted, "If you really want your students to engage in 'higher-order thinking' in math, get them to master basic operations like their times tables first" because when a student "is learning to factor equations in eighth grade, it's a crippling waste of mental energy if he needs to figure out how many times four goes into 20."[155]

He emphasized, "Mastering fundamentals through practice can lift a child's confidence to do harder work." Yet, he observed:

> Unfortunately, a student in a Fuzzy Math program—including *Everyday Mathematics*—is unlikely to master much of anything. The hours of logically linked lessons that old-style math classes spent on practicing operations so that they became second nature to students just are not there. As one local paper, complaining about Fuzzy Math, put it, "Rote learning and the memorization of traditional algorithms appear to have been completely thrown out the window."
>
> Instead of rote learning and memorization, students move haphazardly from one seemingly unconnected topic to another. In Fuzzy Math lingo, it's called "spiraling." On this view, teachers shouldn't use a single method to get addition across to students; they should try lots of approaches—like adding the left-most digits first. That way, the Fuzzy Math approach says, you have a better chance of getting students to understand the concept of addition. In practice, however, trying to teach a host of different methods if students haven't sufficiently mastered any specific one—as is all but inevitable, since they haven't spent much time *practicing* any specific one—can be very confusing. Equally mystifying, *Everyday Mathematics*, like Fuzzy Math programs generally, abruptly introduces concepts like basic algebra that students aren't officially taught until years later. Imagine you're a fourth grader and see in your workbook, right next to a relatively easy

addition word problem, a forbidding algebra exercise you couldn't begin to answer because . . . well, you haven't learned algebra yet. Bewilderment is inevitable.[156]

Clavel gave an example of a fourth-grade word homework problem: "Homer's is selling roller blades at 25 percent off the regular price of $52. Martin's is selling them for one-third off the regular price of $60. Which store is the better buy?" Not an unfair problem on its face, but, he explained:

> Now put yourself in the place of kid who hasn't learned how to multiply quickly, who isn't sure about what a percentage is, and whose knowledge of fractions is meager. The problem will seem forbidding. The homework assignments required way too much reading, too. If you didn't read well, as was the case with many of my kids, it meant that you were going to run into trouble, even if your natural mathematical abilities were strong. The end result: if no adult is around to walk them through the homework assignment, kids will likely dash off a string of guesses and go watch TV.[157]

Math experts have come to the same conclusions as teachers like Clavel.

University of California at Berkeley math professor Hung-Hsi Wu, who was a member of the National Mathematics Advisory Panel, opposed *Everyday Math* because, "It does not pay careful attention to the need of the painstaking build-up of skills, and when this happens in mathematics, you may as well bid farewell to conceptual understanding."[158]

Like Clavel, Wu criticized the curriculum's method of introducing many seemingly disconnected topics before any one topic could be fully learned by students:

The decision by [*Everyday Math*] to dump many topics on children each day, and hope that by chance some of them will stick to the children's minds in the long run, is contrary to the way mathematics should be learned. Mathematics is simple and clear, and its progression is orderly and hierarchical. We want children to learn the most basic things, and learn them well each time, so that they can move to the next stage with a clear understanding of what they have learned, and what they can do next with their new-found knowledge. Some skills and concepts in elementary mathematics are so important (place value, standard algorithms, etc.) that one must not leave the learning of such things to chance. They must be learned, and learned well, and the only way to do this is to isolate them and give children time to absorb them. When you do the standard algorithms as some items among a few dozen that children should know, you are doing public education a disservice.[159]

The *Everyday Math* practices criticized by Clavel and Wu showed up in the classrooms of Sorensen's children.

For example, he said that under *Everyday Math* "they don't teach [addition] in a logical way," going from integer addition to multi-digit addition. Rather, "They'll teach a little bit of addition and then stop after two weeks and go to another topic." The result will be that children "never spend long enough to where they can really get into it." Unfortunately, "that's not the natural way that novice learners learn and it absolutely extinguishes somebody's interest."

When children get confused using *Everyday Math*, Sorensen said, "they'll tell kids we don't really expect you to understand it because we're going to revisit it in six months, so the whole spiral curriculum shortchanges students because you never get in depth."

In addition to the illogical progression of teaching mathematical topics, he sharply criticized *Everyday Math* for its "preference for all the fads that are in vogue in the [university schools of education], like working in groups, no direct instruction, but rather constructivist learning where kids try to figure out the algorithms themselves."

Under constructivist instructional theory, knowledge and skills are not taught to students, but, rather, students are supposed to construct their own knowledge, with teachers acting as mere facilitators. Because they are the constructors of their own knowledge, the theory claims that students will be more motivated to learn.

Tom Loveless, then-director of the Center for Education Policy at the Brookings Institution, has written:

> The premise of constructivism implies that the knowledge students construct on their own, for example, is more valuable than the knowledge modeled for them; told to them; or shown, demonstrated, or explained to them by a teacher. Echoing the historical mantra of progressive education, constructivists argue that the essence of education—its means, ends, and motivating force—should be generated from within the learner, not decided by an external source. The teacher, the textbook, the curriculum, indeed, the entire school and the external authorities it embodies are recast as facilitators in the student's construction of new knowledge, no longer the sources of it.[160]

Constructivism attempts to get away from the so-called "banking theory" of education, which the influential Marxist education theorist Paulo Freire said involves teachers filling the heads of students with content knowledge.[161]

As an engineer and STEM professional, Sorensen says that the intuition of novice learners like students are often wrong and "if you're not provided immediate feedback from expert instructors on incorrect assumptions that you make, it's really hard to root out these false understandings because those neural pathways get set and unless they're corrected you just keep going back to the incorrect understanding."

Loveless pointed out that research suggests that "placing students at the helm of their own intellectual development is generally unproductive," so while student-centered practices "may be defended on ideological grounds—that granting students power, whether it's educationally beneficial or not, is intrinsically good—but empirical support for enhanced learning is weak."[162]

Under group learning, students are grouped into teams and team members work together to learn, achieve common goals, and solve problems. Students are evaluated on the quality of the group product rather than individual work.

Progressive educationists often prefer equity-based group learning to individual learning because they view individual learning as based on competition where talented or hardworking students are rewarded while other students are viewed as losers. Under group learning, the focus is on group performance, not individual performance.

The groups are not organized by ability but purposely include students of different abilities. Students are supposed to not only learn the material themselves, but are asked to assist their fellow group members who may be struggling. This set-up is supposed to stimulate the learning process.

While group learning sounds nice on paper, there is also a distinct utopian tinge to the theory. Indeed, when actually implemented in the classroom, the reality is often much different than the rhetoric of proponents.

"They think the kids are going to help teach themselves," Sorensen said, "but they are novice learners."

He noted, "what happens in group instruction is that one or two kids will do all the work," while other kids in the group engage in "social loafing." Social loafing occurs routinely in group work because a particular person feels less accountability and responsibility for his or her individual effort.

Social loafing is especially prevalent when the product judged and evaluated is that of the group rather than the product of an individual within the group.

"The cynical side of me thinks this is an equity-driven method to share the wealth, intellectual wealth," he observed. "So you can take the grade of the strongest kid in the group and spread it amongst four or five other kids, but it's a false signal because those other kids aren't learning."

In particular, "group learning is viewed as a form of discrimination against gifted learners because they're relied upon to do all the work of the group." He noted, "My kids hated group learning."

In addition to having to shoulder the burden of free riders in their group, higher ability students may be socially coerced into agreeing to a deficient group product (the so-called "ganging-up effect").

Further, group learning takes up a lot of time and with little performance bang. As he concluded, "when it's done, particularly in elementary school, it's just terribly inefficient and you don't get much learning for all the people in the group."

In response to his district's support for *Everyday Math*, he helped found the La Cañada Math Parents grassroots group. The group lobbied against the curriculum, conveying to district officials the view of parents who said the program was confusing; failed to provide enough practice; failed to develop mastery of computational skills and grade-level standards; taught concepts too quickly; and failed to provide differentiated learning opportunities for advancers learners.

He says the parent group "reached out to teachers and found that it wasn't a unanimous feeling [in favor of *Everyday Math*]." The sixth-grade teachers, "who are the most math savvy," said that *Everyday Math* would be implemented in their classrooms "over their dead bodies." When the district eventually approved the adoption of *Everyday Math*, despite the objections of parents, a different more traditional curriculum was adopted just for the sixth grade.

He also said, "teachers who wouldn't go on the record told him, 'We got bullied by these other teachers who said we need to use it.'"

After the district adopted *Everyday Math*, it created an oversight committee for the curriculum, but did not include any members of La Cañada Math Parents. Parents pushed to have the district do a survey of parents to gauge the sentiment of families on the new curriculum. The district, however, refused.

In response to the district's failure to conduct a formal survey specifically on *Everyday Math* and its impact on families, La Cañada Math Parents decided to conduct a survey of parents of elementary-school students in the district. The survey results turned out to be highly revealing.

Only a third of parents believed that K-5 math education in the district was above average.

Forty-two percent of district K-5 parents had problems with *Everyday Math* and less than three out of 10 students were receiving differentiated instruction based on their abilities.

The most eye-opening results were in the area of supplemental instruction.

Fifty-seven percent of students were being tutored or supplemented outside of school, and half of those spent two or more hours a week being tutored in math.

Further, over 60 percent of tutored students had started being tutored in the wake of the adoption of *Everyday Math*. Also, two-thirds of those being tutored in math did not receive tutoring in any other subject.

Sorensen himself has served as a longtime math tutor. "What do you want when kids come in your class?," he asks rhetorically. "You want them to have the fundamentals of arithmetic down," he answers.

He pointed to students who were tutored at the popular after-school Kumon math centers: "The key to Kumon is it uses mastery learning, so you're not allowed to move on to the next subject until you [reach a high performance cut point], and the reason you do that is because of the limitations of how our brain works."

"So," he noted, "you don't want to have to use your working memory to do these intermediate calculations," which must be automatic "so you can save those precious working memory bits for solving higher-level problems." To achieve that automaticity requires "direct instruction and lots of practice."

"I think the false understanding is that conceptual understanding has to come before procedural mastery," when "it's been my observation in the classroom that it's the opposite in many cases—you teach the procedural mastery first and it's only after they've been able to do it that they begin to make the connections to understand what's going on conceptually."

If a progressive curriculum like *Everyday Math* is so ineffective, then why is a district like La Cañada Unified still posting relatively high scores on state standardized tests? Those high scores, he explained, are "not because of the schools, it's because of the parents and supplementation." Indeed, one top math expert told him:

> You will find this counterintuitive phenomenon that sometimes the test scores go up when you implement a really, really bad curriculum because everyone stops using it and they start using outside sources, which many times are better than what they offer in the classroom. So the school will take credit for it and say that [the curriculum] helped our test scores improve, but that doesn't really explain the causality. It was the reaction to [the curriculum].

"So I call this phenomenon the Twinkie effect," he observed. If the school cafeteria started serving Twinkies to everybody, "The conventional wisdom would be, 'Oh, that would be terrible, the kids' teeth would be falling out.'" "No," he countered, "what would happen is parents would take responsibility back and they would send kids to school with lunch or use Uber Eats or whatever to get quality for their kids." In the end, parents are "not going to let them feed Twinkies to their kids, they're going to find out what's good for their kid and feed their kid the right thing."

So, the perverse effect of the district implementing an ineffective curriculum is that it is rewarded with higher test scores, courtesy of the parents paying for more effective outside supplemental instruction for their children, and using those scores to justify the original adoption of the poor curriculum.

He noted that in his school district, the adoption of *Everyday Math* resulted in "people leaving the district, going to private schools, and some left the state."

In an article on his Substack account entitled "Thoughts on Effective Math Instruction," Sorensen summarizes what he sees as ineffective math teaching.

KEY TENETS OF REFORM MATH

Key tenets of ineffective "reform math," according to Sorensen:

- **Emphasis on Conceptual Understanding**—Reform math aspires to develop within the novice learner a deep conceptual understanding of mathematical concepts as opposed to rote learning (a.k.a., *rote memorization*) of math facts and procedures. This is an aspirational goal and those of us who have taught mathematics using both reform math and traditional math approaches and curricula have found no greater conceptual understanding in our students when using reform math approaches. In fact, reform math approaches resulted in more students who not only had no greater conceptual understanding of mathematical concepts, but they could not do basic arithmetic fluently.

- **Students must construct knowledge and discover mathematics for themselves**—Proponents of reform math rely heavily on the constructivist theories of Jerome Bruner and Jean Piaget that emphasized student-centered learning and the theory that novice learners must discover or

---

construct some or all of the essential information they are learning for themselves. Reform math theorists and supporters point to educational research that shows that students who discover a fact, rule, principle, or algorithm for themselves are more likely to remember it in the future. While this may be true, they fail to acknowledge the tradeoffs of discovery learning—it is less efficient than direct instruction, without timely and proper teacher corrections and feedback it can lead to learning incorrect facts, and random control trials show it is far less effective than direct instruction.

- **Group Learning**—*Reform math* supporters champion group work and other forms of collaborative learning. While group learning has its place in the classroom and secondary benefits for children in cultivating group communications and cooperation, studies show it is inefficient compared to direct instruction and poorly designed group work lead to deleterious unintended consequences like *social loafing* and cheating.

- **De-emphasis of Rote Learning and Memorization**—*Reform math* proponents consider basic calculation skills unimportant and advocate instead the use of calculators and other technology for attaining basic numeracy. Time-honored development of basic mathematical skills like memorizing times tables are considered pointless and antithetical to deeper learning, which is only vaguely defined.

- **De-emphasis of Timed Assessments**—Following the advice of math reform high priestess [and Stanford education professor] Jo Boaler, *reform math* proponents believe that timed tests are harmful to students and prefer instead untimed assessments. As Boaler claims on her YouCubed website: "Mathematics facts are important but the memorization of math facts through times table repetition, practice and timed testing is unnecessary and damaging."[163]

In contrast to these ineffective progressive math instructional practices, he believes that traditional math teaching is the secret weapon for student math achievement.

KEY TENETS OF TRADITIONAL MATH

Key tenets of traditional math, according to Sorensen are:

- **Explicit Instruction**—Traditional math practitioners prefer explicit direct instruction by expert instructors to novice learners as opposed to the minimally guided or student-led discovery learning methods preferred by *reform math* advocates.

- **Mastery of Basic Skills**—In the early elementary years, students must learn basic number sense, place value, as well as the fundamental arithmetic operations of addition, subtraction, multiplication and division. Upon these foundational skills, students must learn about fractions and decimals and how to convert between them effortlessly and apply the arithmetic operations to them, measurement, geometry, and data analysis.

- **Procedural Fluency and Automaticity**—Traditional math proponents believe that the memorization of math facts and procedures, which include the standard algorithms, are required to build proficiency and accuracy in mathematical calculations. Another goal of traditional math instructors is *automaticity*—the ability to perform mathematical computations quickly, accurately, and effortlessly, without the need for conscious thought or extensive cognitive effort, called *computational fluency*. The related ability to apply well-memorized procedures and algorithms smoothly and efficiently to solve novel problems is called *procedural fluency*. Computational and procedural fluency, which are often used interchangeably, are seen as the foundation upon which conceptual understanding and problems solving abilities are built. Traditional math practitioners believe practicing math problems is essential

---

to developing understanding, achieving procedural fluency, cultivating accuracy, and extending learning beyond the classroom. Homework that involves practice of skills taught in the classroom, frequently through assignment of problem sets, is regularly assigned in contrast to *reform math* classrooms, where practice is eschewed as "drill and kill," and homework minimized or eliminated altogether.

- **Sequential Progression through Topics**—Traditional math proponents emphasize a sequential and linear progression of mathematical topics, where new concepts are built upon previously learned ones in a structured, hierarchical manner. This approach provides a clear organized framework for students to develop a solid understanding of mathematical concepts.

- **Focus on Mastery of Standard Algorithms**—Traditional math advocates believe the standard algorithms of mathematics such as the long division algorithm should be explicitly taught and practices to mastery before alternate algorithms are taught. They believe that the standard algorithms provide efficient and reliable methods for solving math problems.

- **Emphasis on Accuracy**—Traditional math proponents value correctness and accuracy in mathematical computations. Attention to precision and correct usage of mathematical language and properties is important in developing strong problem-solving abilities and preparing students for higher-level mathematics.

- **Timed Assessments**—Traditional math proponents also do not avoid timed assessments as *reform math* proponents frequently do. In fact, timed assessments are considered critical in the development of mental math and computational fluency in the early elementary grades.[164]

He noted that high-performing countries such as Singapore, South Korea, and Japan use traditional math instructional methods.

Given the predominance of progressive reform math instruction in American classrooms, it is no surprise that countries that use more effective traditional math instruction are way ahead of the United States.

For example, he noted, "the gap between Singapore and the U.S. is equivalent to three years of math education."

The end result of ineffective math instruction is not just tragedy for individual students, but, in addition, it is a catastrophe for the American economy. As he noted, "deficient math and science education leads to a dearth of qualified kids for the needs in the economy, such as in high tech." Without qualified American workers, businesses are "going to import workers from other countries or outsource it to other countries which can do it."

He observed "it's doubly bad" because "you're making a claim that provides false hope to kids that they can get access to these jobs, and you're actually crippling them in their ability to do so."

The irony, he noted, is that the U.S. has "what many consider is the best college and graduate school system in the world, but many of our kids can't get access to it."

Even when young people do enter higher education, many are surprised by their lack of college preparedness. He observed, "you're not doing these kids any favors by lowering standards and dumbing down curriculum, you're just giving them a false promise and then they're going to hit reality when they get to college."

Despite his mathematical expertise, his school district ignored his complaints and the complaints of his fellow parents and adopted an ineffective math curriculum. In such a situation, what are parents to do?

"Parents," he advised, "should respond as they always have when benighted math education polices are adopted by government education 'experts'—take control of your child's math education."

He bluntly urged parents: "Decide that you will not leave the fate of your child's math future, and the potential careers it unlocks, to public school administrators and paid math education consultants christened in the cesspool that is American schools of education."

Rather, "Seek out alternative paths, and if you are stuck in a public school or a progressive private school that uses the latest fashionable math education approach," then "supplement your child's classroom math education with outside mathematics through one of the many math enrichment centers, online programs, or private tutors."

In other words, when the education blob proves intractable, then parents need to vote with their feet.

CHAPTER 11

A Professional Math Tutor Reveals Why Students in an Affluent School District Are Failing

Pointing to ineffective math instruction in schools, math tutor Michael Malione warns: "As long as they keep messing up the younger kids, it's just a matter of time before no one will be able to get to algebra in the eighth grade because the kids won't know enough. That's why it's really important to keep your eye on the younger grades and what they're doing there."

Born in Oakland, California, Malione is the son of two artists—a musician father and a dancer mother. From a young age, however, he had very different interests than his parents.

"I wanted to be a scientist," he said, so "I gravitated to math and science." "I was really good at it," he smiled, "and it wasn't something my parents could tell me what to do because it was just sort of foreign to them."

He attended San Francisco's Lowell High School, one of California's top academic public schools. He became a National Merit Scholar and then entered Harvard University, where he majored in chemistry and physics.

After Harvard, he moved back to California and got a masters degree in engineering from Stanford University and worked for companies such as Pixar and Industrial Light and Magic.

His first teaching experience came when he was hired as an adjunct faculty member at Academy of Art University in San Francisco. He taught a number of classes, including basic core math and physics.

After his children were born, he became a stay-at-home dad and did tutoring on the side. He eventually became a math teacher at Piedmont High School in the affluent city of Piedmont, which is totally surrounded by the city of Oakland.

During the 2019-20 school year, when he taught at Piedmont High, he recalled, "I really became aware of how far things had fallen in the way math is taught."

He immediately noticed that the math curriculum at the school, College Preparatory Math (CPM), was not very rigorous or demanding when compared to classic math textbooks from his childhood.

Referencing one classic text, he said, "They would have three sections—A, B, C—and the A problems were considered very straightforward, you're doing what we just showed you how to do." The B problems would be harder, "you have to think maybe two steps ahead or beyond what's just right in front of you." The C problems pushed students "to think about it and kind of do some discovery on their own to answer them."

In contrast, he said, "when I looked at CPM, I never saw anything more than the first half of the As."

Consequently, he noticed, for example, that his students "couldn't do fractions and decimals fluently." And because students had not been taught important basics, less emphasis was then put on more difficult types of problems.

Many parents also felt that CPM shortchanged students in the amount of material covered.

One parent said, "My observation is that this curriculum is more confusing and less comprehensive." This parent's daughters complained about "how little is covered in CPM textbooks and what superficial foundation they provide in math."[165]

Which topics are inadequately covered in CPM? As an example, he pointed to mixture problems.

"So a mixture problem," he explained, would be something like "you have a 60% sulfuric solution and a 10% sulfuric solution, how much of the lower solution would I need to make a 50% solution." Or, "My nice coffee beans cost me $3 a pound and my cheap beans cost me 75 cents a pound, so how much should I mix to create 10 pounds of a mixture that cost me $2 a pound."

"These mixture problems," he noted, "were put into a section that was considered almost optional . . . and it was a section that maybe we'll get to it, maybe we won't and my understanding is our school never did get to it." Thus, math topics that "were considered important are now considered almost too hard."

What is shocking about such a revelation is that Piedmont is a high-income city with supposedly high quality public schools. When asked if that was a surprise to him, he replied, "It was to me at the time."

One of the key facets of CPM is its reliance on group learning. Dr. David Kristofferson, a retired scientist who has spent many years as a teacher and tutor, taught high school math using CPM and noted, "The program strongly encourages group work over individual study."[166]

"Students," he has written, "are typically placed in groups of four in their classroom and are given defined roles within their group: 'Resource Manager,' 'Facilitator,' 'Recorder/Reporter,' and 'Task Manager.'"[167]

Ideally, "Students have active discussions about the material and work on group problems in class versus passively listening to lectures, taking notes, and only working actively when they do homework alone after school."[168]

In a typical CPM lesson, "Each textbook section begins with a series of guided questions that lead students to discover a new math concept if they answer the questions correctly and in order."

According to Kristofferson:

> Teachers are supposed to move around the class
> from group to group, answering questions from
> each group and making sure that students are
> on task. Lecturing is kept to a minimum. This
> is in agreement with the "learning by doing"
> philosophy. Current teaching practice tends to
> denigrate lecturing calling a lecturer a "sage on
> the stage," with the implication that lecturing
> stokes the ego of the teacher instead of really
> instructing the student.
>
> . . . If the student groups are well struc-
> tured, the better students help those in their
> group who struggle with math, and everyone
> benefits. The good students benefit because,
> paradoxically, there is no better way to learn a
> subject than to teach it. The less mathematically-
> inclined students get help from their peers,
> which is often less intimidating than asking a
> question from a teacher.[169]

Of course, the real-world implementation of CPM often
differed markedly from this idealized learning process. Kristofferson wrote, "Putting pre-teens or teens who 'hate math' into
groups results in a major 'classroom management' challenge for
a teacher." Specifically, "The group conversation is often on any
popular teenage topic other than mathematics when the teacher
is not watching."[170]

Thus, in a higher-performing classroom, "if a group is able
to finish the guided questions, then they learn the lesson for
the day," while, "In a poorer class, however, the teacher often
has to answer the same questions repeatedly for each group and
may eventually decide to stop the class and lecture for a while
on the topic."[171]

Kristofferson cited a teacher at one high school where CPM
was being tried who "tended to lecture at the beginning of each

class" and that teacher's students "were appreciative of this lecture effort while those in classes where the teachers followed the standard self-discovery prescription were often frustrated." One student in a classroom where the teacher used the discovery method exclusively "was upset with the teacher's 'hands-off' approach, commented to me, 'Don't they get paid to teach?'"[172]

While teachers are supposedly paid to teach, Kristofferson observed, "a burned out teacher can use the CPM program as an excuse to coast." Thus, "the students are supposed to work themselves, so 'get in your groups, open your book to section X, and do problems Y to Z' is a very minimal teaching effort required."[173]

Finally, Kristofferson pointed to CPM's troubling use of so-called "group tests":

> [S]tudents in CPM classes also engage in a practice called "group tests." All four students in a group work collaboratively on a test. At the end of the period, the teacher randomly picks one of the group's four test papers, grades it later, and then assigns that grade to everyone in the group.
>
> The first time this happens during the school year, some of the groups will have a paper selected from the weakest student in the group, and everyone in that group might end up with a bad grade. During subsequent group tests, the better students in the group will frantically check that everyone's test papers have the same answers, so that they do not "get screwed over" a second time. Parents tend to shake their heads incredulously when they learn about this practice, and I can't blame them.[174]

Many of the CPM deficiencies that Kristofferson described manifested themselves in Malione's classroom.

When students were conversing with each other, ostensibly to discover knowledge, he said, "What I saw was off-topic chatter."

"They'd spend 80 percent of their time doing off-topic chatter," he recalled, "and 20 percent of the time doing the math they were supposed to do."

"The group learning just invited them to talk about whatever they wanted," he observed, "and I would come around to try to steer them more to the topic, but usually what I saw was maybe one minute of attention from them when I walked by, then I would go to the next group, and they would go back to whatever they were talking about."

When he was the teacher, "it made it very hard for me to know who actually knew how to do this and who didn't." Further, "there would be some kids who were so easily distracted." So this method of teaching made it difficult to evaluate individual student performance and made it more difficult for many students to learn anything.

Shockingly, based on the curriculum, when children had questions, he said, "I'm not supposed to answer questions, I'm supposed to just encourage them to figure it out and instruct them on procedures."

When students would raise their hands and say they were confused about something and ask for an explanation, he said that he would explain it to them, "but technically, I'm told, I'm not even supposed to do that," according to "the curriculum and the way it's intended to be used."

Rather, students are "supposed to have this productive struggle where I just give them little hints and say try this and then leave them to it." Unfortunately, for students, "that's very frustrating when they don't even know what they're supposed to be finding [and discovering]."

Proponents of discovery learning believe that the process of discovering knowledge leads to deeper understanding. However, he said, "It puts all the attention on how do we do it and takes away from practice."

"Somehow, this idea is that if they really deeply understand how to do it, they'll be able to do it."

"So there's this idea," he said, "that by discovering it, by being led into it, that this will help them understand it so then they know it and then they won't forget it." Thus, "you're going to discover it on your own through some exercise you do where you don't know what you're supposed to find and you're led down a path that's supposed to make it apparent to you, so then you are asked to put it together, given what's now apparent to you."

"There's a number of problems with that," he said: "One, they never really put it together, so how are they going to remember it if they didn't actually put it together for themselves? And two, even if they put it together it's very concrete, and hasn't been abstracted in a way that they're able to then turn into something they can just do."

In other words, a picture is concrete, while multiplying numerators and denominators in fractions is abstract, but it is the abstract operation that allows students to do that operation efficiently and more effectively.

Malione pointed out, "you can't do it all with discovery."

"Discovery is great for some illumination and it's helpful," he said, "but you can't do everything that way because it takes away from the actual learning of the facts and getting the fluency you need." "So when you try to do everything that way, they learn nothing."

The time inefficiency of discovery learning results in schools deciding that "we're trying to cover too many things, we need to cover less."

So, "the way you get to know how to do it is by saying, well, here's how you do it, try it, and then we're going to do a bunch of them." Then, "if you're informed by having done 20, when the explanation comes of how it works then it makes more sense."

Not surprisingly, discovery learning "doesn't really work if the kids aren't motivated and they just want to goof off." Also, he said that the coverage of the material "is only so superficial."

Kristofferson summarizes the discovery-learning/group-learning problems with CPM:

In summary the biggest problems with CPM are the lack of explanations, worked example problems in textbooks, and insufficient practice problems. The first two omissions are by design because each group is supposed to discover the concepts through guided questions. Worked examples would circumvent this process.

However, if a group does not "get" the topic and fails to complete the guided problems in class, they are left with nothing to explain how they should do the homework. Essentially the student has a textbook with only questions and little or no explanations. This is a significant problem in classes with weaker math students who are absent from class. They have nothing to refer to at home unless the teacher puts additional material on the Web. However, this means the students have to navigate to other sources instead of just being able to use their textbooks.[175]

After his stint teaching at Piedmont High Malione then started tutoring students.

At first he got mostly middle school children, but then elementary school children started to come to him because their parents were saying, "my kids are not learning things they should be learning." He said that 90 percent of his tutoring clients came from Piedmont.

For instance, he said that elementary school students seemingly had not been taught how to multiply fractions.

Students were taught how to add and subtract fractions, "but when it came to just multiplying, dividing, and understanding what fractions are, they would just get dumbfounded to the point where they just don't know what to do when they see it."

The big problem he saw in the way that math was taught to young children in Piedmont schools was an overemphasis on so-called conceptual understanding over simple numerical operation.

Take, for example, multiplying two fractions, such as ½ x ¾. Instead of simply multiplying the numerators, 1 x 3, and the denominators, 2 x 4, to get the right answer of 3/8, teachers had children draw pictures to illustrate how the problem would be solved.

He said that children were told by their teachers to draw a rectangle and split the rectangle into parts and then shade the parts to represent ½ and ¾, with the result that the shaded parts show "three parts out of eight to make the whole, so the whole thing is tied to looking a picture and counting instead of just multiplying."

Often students were forced to use this picture-drawing technique multiple times before they were ever told that they could solve the problem just by the numerical operation of multiplying the numerators and the denominators. That operation "became a side note." Thus, students would not remember "oh yeah, you just have to multiply."

Teachers would defend this instructional technique by saying, "Well, this is conceptual understanding." He retorted, "Fine, you showed it to them once and then you get on with doing it symbolically," but the teachers would say, "no, because too many kids don't understand it, so we have to show them and this is the way they can understand it."

Students are "supposed to be taught to draw the picture, so the idea is that as soon as you see a [fraction problem] you draw a picture." He shakes his head saying: "We're going to draw a picture every time we're given 10 problems with fractional multiplication, when you could do them in your head? We're going to take time and draw 10 pictures and draw lines and shade? That's insane."

Not only is this instructional technique ineffective, it is also highly inefficient.

"It does take a long time," he observed, "that's a big problem and that's why they had to remove all of this content because it takes so long that they ended up saying we have to remove this because it's just too much."

As usual, children are the big losers when adults place their idealized teaching methods over the real-world learning problems they cause to students. The students' math struggles were not their fault, but the fault of ineffective math instruction.

Malione would have students he tutored who "don't remember how to multiply two digit numbers because they never practiced it enough," and when "the work is getting harder to the point that they don't want to draw pictures every time."

He would also see students "who haven't been taught that A over B and A divided by B are the same thing."

"I would work with them," he said, "and they would get stuck because there were things they didn't know."

Students with weaker math skills were the ones who suffered most. These students, he said, "are the ones who are completely lost and they're not getting the step-by-step guidance early on." "They're just treading water," he lamented, "and they don't even know how to tread water well."

"They could be learning more in the early grades," he noted, "but they're not," and "some are frustrated because they're struggling and they don't know why."

Like Sugi Sorensen, who outlined effective math instructional methods in the previous chapter, Malione said he finds children who are struggling but "could do just fine doing math the traditional way, and the traditional way helps them a lot."

Specifically, "I would say that you need explicit instruction, and you can have some discovery [learning], but the only way you're going to cover all the content without removing a bunch of it is with good and directed explicit instruction," which means "a logical step-by-step development of increasingly difficult concepts and involved procedures."

For his tutoring, he used a learning tool called Beast Academy, which describes itself as a "rigorous math curriculum" that uses "tough problems" so students "gain a skill stack that extends far beyond math alone."[176]

"I have a big success story," he said. In his tutoring, he had a sixth grader whose parent reached out to him "because they felt the math was confusing in the course and the student was struggling."

He discovered that the student really had a talent for math, but "just didn't know how to put the pieces together because it wasn't being covered well, and I came in and would work with him once a week and they made incredible progress, like a year of math in the time that I spent one semester with him."

While Malione is making progress with individual students, most other students, even if they come from advantaged backgrounds, are ending up befuddled and frustrated by the math instruction they are receiving in school.

Over the years, his opinion about math standards, curricula, and instruction has gone from "this doesn't really look good to me to I don't see how this is going to work to, oh my god, what have we done?"

"This is crazy," he says. Unfortunately, many children and their parents think so, too.

CHAPTER 12
A Parent's Fight Against an Ineffective Math Curriculum

"It was really during the pandemic," said California mom Rebeka Sinclair, "being on Zoom with my young children, seeing what they were learning, why they were learning it, and how they were learning it that really woke me up to the fact that as a parent I am their primary educator."

"So where I see weaknesses in our academic program," she emphasized, "I have definitely been vocal, I am a leader at our school, and I've brought my concerns to the superintendent."

Sinclair, who is profiled in the previous reading section of this book, had a very different experience with her local public school when it came to mathematics.

While her children's school in Orange County, California had done an excellent job in incorporating effective science-of-reading curriculum and teaching methods into the school's education program, the school insisted on pushing an ineffective math curriculum that was not supported by the science of mathematics.

Her children's school used a math curriculum called Bridges in Mathematics, which has been favored by progressive educators. Indeed, the Bridges' website is replete with progressive buzzwords.

"Inquiry-based and student-centered," says the website, "Bridges focuses on developing mathematical reasoning while creating an inclusive and equitable learning community for all students" and "brings focus to representation, provides guidance for creating an inclusive learning environment, and includes revised tasks that support equity."[177]

What does a classroom using the Bridges curriculum look like? According to the company:

> In a Bridges classroom, students gather evidence, explain their results, and develop respect for others' opinions. Teachers encourage students to employ multiple strategies when solving problems. They foster student initiative by providing opportunities to work in pairs, discuss in small groups, or share with the whole class. As a result, students develop positive math identities while building problem-solving skills, conceptual understanding, and procedural fluency.[178]

While this description paints a utopian picture of math instruction and learning, Sinclair said that the reality was much different.

"The progressive trend is the transition from direct instruction to student-led inquiry," she explained.

According to the Glossary of Education Reform, direct instruction is defined as: "1) instructional approaches that are structured, sequenced, and led by teachers, and/or 2) the presentation of academic content to students by teachers, such as in a lecture or demonstration. In other words, teachers are 'directing' the instructional process or instruction is being 'directed' at students."[179]

In contrast, one STEM education professor defined student-led inquiry learning as emphasizing, "a student's role in the learning process and asks them to engage with an idea or topic in an active way rather than sitting and listening to a teacher." Specifically, "To learn a topic, students explore resources, ask questions and share ideas."[180]

Under inquiry learning, the teacher takes on the role as facilitator rather than instructor and "helps students apply new concepts to different contexts, which allows them to discover knowledge for themselves by exploring, experiencing and discussing as they go."[181]

Thus, "The overall goal of an inquiry-based approach is for students to make meaning of what they are learning about and to understand how a concept works in a real-world context."[182]

Sinclair said that under student-led inquiry learning in her children's school "there are no timed tests; there's no rote memorization; there's a huge focus on students feeling good about math and seeing themselves in the work and open-ended problems, but they are not given a strong background in the mathematical algorithms that are needed to advance to higher levels of math, so that's very concerning."

She is especially concerned about "the lack of assessments of basic math facts."

"I am not seeing," she observed, "my students come home with timed tests, or preparing for timed tests with flashcards, practicing these math problems over and over to try to become proficient."

Instead, she sees, "very lengthy and somewhat open-ended word problems, which for some types of learners can be very beneficial, but without a strong mathematical foundation they can be very difficult to solve, which might even create a lack of confidence around math."

Without "a solid foundation of math fact proficiency, students are not going to be able to advance to the more abstract algorithmic type of thinking."

She pushed her school on the lack of timed tests in math, but "one response I get is that everyone has a calculator in their pocket." "I think that is such a flawed response," she warned, "because the brain needs to be wired in a certain way to handle higher level mathematical thinking and without those neurological connections then students have the potential to be completely lost and behind when you get to the upper [math] echelons and you are seeing that so clearly in the decimation of math scores across the state and the country."

Her dissatisfaction with the student-led inquiry learning is not just the unhappiness of one parent. Research evidence supports her view.

Referring to student-led instruction, active learning, active inquiry, and collaborative instruction, former U.S. assistant secretary of education Williamson Evers and former U.S. Department of Education senior policy advisor Ze'ev Wurman noted, "evidence from the 1950s through recent times shows that this way of teaching math is ineffective."[183]

A study by researchers from the University of Southern California and from Australia reviewed the research on both direct instruction and student-led inquiry learning. Regarding how inquiry learning is used in math classes, they explain:

> The partially guided approach has been given various names, including discovery learning, problem-based learning, inquiry learning, experiential learning, and constructivist learning. Continuing the math example, students receiving partial instructional guidance may be given a new type of problem and asked to brainstorm possible solutions in small groups with or without prompts or hints. Then there may be class discussion of the various groups' solutions, and it could be quite some time before the teacher indicates which solution is correct. Through this process of trying to solve the problem and discussing different students' solutions, each student is supposed to discover the relevant mathematics.[184]

According to the study, research shows that under a student-led inquiry-learning method students "often become lost and frustrated, and their confusion can lead to misconceptions." Further, "because false starts (in which students pursue misguided hypotheses) are common in such learning situations, unguided discovery is most often inefficient."[185]

"In real classrooms," the study observed, "often only the brightest and most well-prepared students make the discovery," while many students "simply become frustrated." Other students "may disengage, others may copy whatever the brightest students are doing—either way, they are not actually discovering anything."[186]

Also, students may believe they have discovered the correct solution, "but they are mistaken and so they learn a misconception that can interfere with later learning and problem solving." Even after being shown the right answer, "a student is likely to recall his or her discovery—not the correction."[187]

Inquiry learning is also time inefficient: "What can be taught directly in a 25-minute demonstration and discussion, followed by 15 minutes of independent practice with corrective feedback by a teacher may take several class periods to learn via minimally guided projects and/or problem solving."[188]

Finally, using minimally guided instruction, "can increase the achievement gap," with research showing that using such a teaching method "produced measurable loss of learning."[189]

The study's bottom-line findings were unequivocal:

> Decades of research clearly demonstrate that *for novices* (comprising virtually all students), direct, explicit instruction is more effective than partial guidance. So, when teaching new content and skills to novices, teachers are more effective when they provide explicit guidance accompanied by practice and feedback, not when they require students to discover many aspects of what they must learn.[190]

For Sinclair, her school's student-led inquiry-learning math curriculum did not work for her children. Therefore, like other parents interviewed for this book, she had to enroll them in supplemental after-school math programs.

"We actually enroll our children in a completely separate math curriculum," she said. "They go to their public school and then they are enrolled in a fully accredited math class that we do at home on Zoom."

Her oldest son "is particularly advanced" and "he does not learn anything new at school when it comes to math." Rather, "the learning that really challenges him to grow as a mathematician occurs at home with the separate program in which we have enrolled him."

She is not alone among parents with whom she is acquainted. "I know that a lot of parents in our community spend a lot of resources on math tutors or Kumon [after-school] math, and different math programs," she said.

While she and her fellow parents in her district can afford these supplemental programs and resources, she worries about disadvantaged families. "It's really unfortunate," she observed, "because without that [supplemental] support I think students in lower income areas are really handicapped without strong mathematical foundations."

In addition, one can wonder about the face value of seemingly high state standardized test scores at more affluent public schools. Are those high scores the result of the teaching at the school or are they the result of higher income parents using their resources to purchase supplemental instructional services for their children to make up for the teaching deficiencies at the school? She believes the latter.

She said that the same math curriculum is used in her affluent city and in a nearby economically disadvantaged city in the same school district. The schools in the disadvantaged city actually receive more government education funding. Yet, Sinclair noted, at her children's school, "I think we are in the mid to high 80s in math proficiency," but district-wide, "only 48 percent of students are meeting math [grade-level] benchmarks."

That data "definitely suggests that it is parental support and the community that's driving those test scores."

One of the other key problems that she sees in the way math is taught at her children's school is the emphasis on equity, which means the same outcome for all students. The Bridges curriculum, for example, says that it "supports equity" and aims to create "an equitable learning environment for all students."

Equity has become a ubiquitous justification for any progressive program. Yet, real-life students feel the negative impacts of this equity mindset.

"I think that the focus on equity of outcomes in our education system has decimated rigor," she said. Unfortunately, "the focus on equity of outcomes is pervasive in California K through 12 public schools, and our superintendent would use the word a lot."

However, she observed, "Not all students will progress to the same finish line of high school math and that completely contradicts the whole movement around equity, where we should have equal outcomes at the end."

In her children's elementary school, "they're all moving in lockstep together, even though you have some very high aptitude students who can handle a lot more and students at the lower end that may need extra support." As the example of her older son demonstrates, "unfortunately, the way math is approached in our school ultimately handicaps students at the high end."

She faults the equity mentality for the lack of gifted-and-talented program funding in her district. She says, "there's no budget line for gifted and talented" in her district budget, but "we spend $78 million on special education students." So, she noted, there is significant funding going to challenged students "and very little to none going to students at the high end."

"For every student to feel good and to not feel bad about math," she observed, "the bar needs to be lowered," so in the name of equity "you can't have these small groups of students that have accelerated learning in elementary school."

"It is teaching and allocating resources to the lowest common denominator," she warned, "and it prevents acceleration and challenge and the acknowledgement that these higher performing students deserve similar resource allocation and a curriculum that really serves their learning."

She pointed out that the progressive ideology of policymakers in Sacramento "tells textbook manufacturers how to frame curriculum since California is the fifth largest market for textbook manufacturers." Thus, she observed, "teachers who could be very well meaning, even moderates, not necessarily super progressive, are teaching a very progressive curriculum and philosophy without even knowing it."

Given the challenges that parents and their children face, Sinclair makes a number of recommendations for moms and dads.

"Number one," she said, "is to take full ownership over your child's education" and "it's not just academics, it's also heart, mind, and character," including "the way they view the world and the way they view our country."

"Once you have that mindset," she noted, "you do research to understand why they're learning what they're learning and what's happening in our schools." Then, "you will have more confidence to steer the educational ship for your kids."

Despite the fact that she is aware of the decline of "rigor for our kids, we are still sending them to our neighborhood public school."

"We love our teachers as people," she said, but "we're also advocating for change at the same time to hopefully benefit students."

Thus, rather than abandoning the public schools, she has chosen to stay and fight for a better education, not just for her children, but for all children. Parents, though, must band together to succeed in effecting change: "I feel like one parent's voice alone can't bring about change, it takes a number of parents getting involved in a certain issue."

CHAPTER 13
A College Math Professor Describes the Disastrous End Product of Ineffective K-12 Math

"I'd say that particularly in math I think America does a pretty bad job of it in general," observed Frank.

Frank, whose name has been changed to protect his anonymity, is a faculty member in the math department at a California college. He is on the receiving end of the students who have gone through the K-12 math instruction described by Sugi Sorensen, Mike Malione, and Rebecca Sinclair. And what he sees is both shocking and frightening.

"Foundational knowledge is really the key to success in math and science," he said. Specifically, "foundational knowledge would be like algebra, geometry, and word problems that really exercise your skills."

Unfortunately, in the U.S., "foundational knowledge is generally lacking because that's not the main goal of education."

He teaches calculus at his college and said that the lack of algebra knowledge is "the number one deficiency and it's chronic."

"So when a student comes to college," he observed, "without algebra skills and without analytical skills there is really no hope." "It causes a lot of problems because that person is not ready to be educated at the level of calculus."

On a more granular level, Frank sees the reduction in rigor in K-12 math education in things like word problems.

Word problems have, for years, been one of the most challenging exercises given to students. With the decline in foundational knowledge and skills, however, the rigor of word problems has decreased. For example, the breadth of the types of word problems is becoming more limited.

"So, working on a word problem is supposed to invigorate your analytical skills," said Frank, but, "if you work on the same word problem that you've seen before, and they just change the numbers, there is no educational value since you're not learning to analyze things, you are just learning to react to things that you already know will be coming at you."

Because students are not exposed to a wide variety of word problems, Frank noted that when he designs his own tests, "I need to be really careful not to test creativity because people aren't used to that," so, "it needs to be pretty much the problem that they've seen with the numbers changed."

So, what does Frank believe is the goal of K-12 education?

Unfortunately, rather than teaching students the foundational knowledge and skills they need to succeed, "the education system is used to socialize people more than in the past." Further, "the system is set up for [measuring] success using other parameters, like getting people through," while actual education "comes in as a secondary goal."

Success in American education is measured by "achieving a high number of students passing from one level to the next," so "the deans or the principals will put pressure on high school teachers who tell us they're under a lot of pressure to get students passed by any means." Thus, "if a student fails a test, it's not a problem, they can take it again."

As a consequence, "the idea of just passing means that you'll learn enough to pass and the knowledge is never really learned and retained for future reference."

Therefore, "I have tried to impart to my students that every time you make a mistake, and this is true of life as well, there is a cost to the wrong, and when you've prepared just enough, with a lot of mistakes, you can pass," but, "at some point you are going to pay for your mistakes."

"A company can't keep losing money," he observed, because "they have to be a for-profit organization." In the Silicon Valley, for example, "there's a lot of competition for getting products that succeed, so you can't have a failing workforce trying to support your success."

Jobs in high tech "are really difficult and when you're a software engineer you really have to drive towards perfection because every mistake that you make will show at some point and cost the company, so you're under a lot of stress to be perfect."

Unfortunately, "if you have an education system that is not encouraging that," and instead the system easily forgives mistakes, students will collide with a totally different reality in high tech because "that is not the way Silicon Valley works."

"They can't allow mistakes to pile up upon mistakes," he says, "and they can't have people who have that kind of attitude, so we're not producing the kinds of students and graduates that Silicon Valley needs."

Just how lacking are today's young people?

One indicator of students' lack of preparedness in math, according to Frank, is the high attrition rate in college math classes.

In his experience, a regular college math class "would have attrition of, I'd say, at least 50 percent." In a pre-calculus class "where the rubber meets the road for some students, I wouldn't be surprised to see attrition rates of 70 to 80 percent."

Such attrition is unsurprising because if a student has inadequate algebra skills, "you're going to be on quicksand in calculus, you're going to fail every step along the way."

In terms of preparedness at his college, even among those who do not drop out of class, he thinks, "maybe a large per-

centage of the remaining students aren't really prepared, either."
However, the predictable testing methods used in his college
"allows them to pass," but, "if you really threw them curveballs
that you will see in other countries, I don't think that many of
our students can actually pass."

If his course was being taught in a high-performing math
country like Singapore, Frank said, "I wouldn't be surprised if
85 percent [of his students] were not able to pass it at all."

What is heartbreaking, he says, is that many of his students
are eager for a chance at a STEM career and they really want
to learn, but "the system has failed them in the past so they're
not ready."

"That lack of preparedness," he explained, "just propagates
up and up and up, even to upper division classes where, without
a curve, pretty much everybody will fail."

And, sadly, "You can see that the companies don't want
these graduates." "So a company in Silicon Valley that's special-
izing in artificial intelligence wants heavy hitters," he said, "and
you're never going to be a part of that."

Like a domino, though, the ineffectiveness of K-12 math
education ends up affecting the teaching practices in higher education.

Pressure is placed on college math faculty to pass and give
higher grades to students even if they do not merit them. Frank
observes that the result is not good for anyone:

> I know someone who routinely gave the bor-
> derline grades the next higher grade, arbitrari-
> ly, like if you got 67% he'll give it a C instead of
> a D. And his point was that nobody was going
> to complain about that. But you're just passing
> a D student to the next level, who will be sure
> to fail at the next level if some rigor is main-
> tained there. The problem is that these students
> become part of your failure rate, so somebody
> else passed along their failure rate to you and
> now you have the problem that this student

is going to fail. And that's part of my failure. This is how the problem cascades up the chain and you have a failure rate that goes up and up and up. Then you might be teaching an upper division course in some STEM level like organic chemistry and the students don't even have the basics down because they have been pushed along.

Because of this phenomenon of failing up, college administrators shift the focus from what students do not know to concepts like equity, which means that all students must have the same outcomes regardless of their knowledge and merit.

In discussions with administrators, Frank estimates that "no more than 10 percent of our discussion is probably about [what students know]." Instead, "A lot of energy and discussion is about equity and there's a huge emphasis on success rate," which is basically the rate of students who pass.

Faculty "are measured by success rate and student reviews, and student reviews, in my opinion, are highly correlated with getting high grades."

For a faculty member to stand up for rigor would "introduce a lot of craziness into my life." For instance, "if I didn't allow retakes [on tests] I myself could be in trouble, where I would have a lot of issues with my dean and with the administration." So, "you have to really walk a fine line between rigor and the expectations that are placed on you."

In the end, he says, "Education is hard for everyone—it's hard to learn, it's hard to learn new things, and you have to work hard at it." What is important is the "orientation of the institutions, their mission, and also the culture of value that's attached to education itself."

If our educational institutions were focused on prioritizing excellence and pushing students to achieve to high levels, then that hard work of education would be worth it. In contrast, though, he concludes, "the system actually encourages and rewards lack of rigor."

Students, the economy, and America itself are all the victims of the country's education failures.

SECTION 4: CONCLUSION

CHAPTER 14
Reform Recommendations

Why are students failing to achieve their highest potential? This book has examined the reasons why schools are failing our children.

For example, too many schools are putting political ideology over what works, whether it be a misguided equity agenda that seeks to dumb down learning to a lowest common denominator or the blocking of successful learning methods from being used in the classroom due to philosophical prejudice.

In reading and math, progressive curricula and instructional methods are being used in schools across the country in intellectual defiance of empirical evidence showing that they are ineffective and are damaging children.

The individuals profiled in this book have fought against these ideological and ineffective programs in various ways.

For example, Oredola Taylor, the Minnesota mom who grew up in West Africa, joined with parents at her children's school to battle school district officials who were intent on watering down classroom rigor in the school in order to adhere to an equity ideology that could not countenance a mostly minority school from achieving at a higher level than other schools in the district.

When his children's school district pushed deficient curricula in the schools, parent and JPL engineer Sugi Sorensen helped form a local parent advocacy group that fought for effective evidence-based reading and math curricula.

Parent and former teacher Missy Purcell became a one-person army fighting her school district for better reading instruction for children.

The efforts of these parents exemplify a trend across the country of moms and dads taking the fight for better education and higher achievement for their children directly to their school boards and state policymakers.

In Oakland, California, which has a terrible history of failing to improve the learning of children, parents are rising up.

Families in Oakland have discovered just how badly the city's schools have failed their children with the help of the nonprofit organization Families in Action for Quality Education, which, according to the *San Francisco Chronicle*, helps "predominantly Black and brown parents better understand student and district data and advocate for their children's education."[191]

In 2022-23, just 17 percent of African-American students in Oakland schools met grade-level reading standards on the state test, while just over 10 percent met grade-level math standards on the state test.[192]

In that same school year, 23 percent of Latino students in Oakland scored at grade-level in reading, while only 14 percent scored at grade-level in math.[193]

Kimi Kean, a former school principal and the head of Families in Action for Quality Education, said that after unraveling reading and math data parents are shocked and angry.

She said: "Our families are not taking it anymore."[194]

Families, she told the *Chronicle*, are fed up with the school board and special interests focusing more on political issues instead of setting and achieving better academic outcomes for students.[195]

Citing the school board's focus on Israel-Hamas war in Gaza, Oakland mom Stephisha Ycoy-Walton said: "There's no reason as a parent I should walk in a board meeting that was canceled abruptly and was adjourned because of political activities taking place on the other side of the world. If that is a major topic of a school board meeting, we are misdirected."[196]

Therefore, the *Chronicle* noted, "After decades of administrative dysfunction, budget deficits, low test scores, teacher strikes, school closure debates and other upheaval, these parents say they are organizing to refocus funding public meetings and political priorities on reading, writing and arithmetic."[197]

Families in Action is pushing the Oakland city council and the school board to double the literacy and math proficiency rates of African American and Latino students over the next decade and increase the proportion of students eligible to attend state universities.[198]

As parents organize and demand better academic outcomes for their children, they need to understand what works and what does not when it comes to improving reading and math learning.

School boards adopting lofty academic goals will mean nothing if the means to achieve those goals—evidence-based curricula and instructional methods—are not also part of the plan.

The parents and teachers profiled in this book, such as Missy Purcell, Kate Bowers, and Sugi Sorensen, have detailed what works when it comes to reading and math learning.

In addition, newly activated parents should take note of the recommendations by organizations such as the National Council on Teacher Quality, which has been fighting for evidence-based educational policies, such as the science of reading, for years.

REFORM RECOMMENDATIONS FOR SCHOOL DISTRICTS

The National Council on Teacher Quality recommend that school boards and districts:

- Be strategic in recruiting new teachers. To the extent possible, focus hiring efforts on teachers from preparation programs adequately teaching scientifically based reading instruction, or from stronger programs in your areas.

- Prioritize partnerships for field experiences with programs committed to teaching scientifically based reading instruction.

- Provide professional development opportunities for teachers already in the classroom who were not prepared in scientifically based reading instruction.

- Review, select, and carefully implement high-quality reading curricula approved by your state or other external reviewers along with aligned, job-embedded, high-quality professional development to skillfully implement the curricula, and share your curriculum resources with teacher preparation partners.[199]

NCTQ recommendations for state policymakers include:

- Set specific, explicit, and comprehensive preparation standards for scientifically based reading instruction. These standards need to explicitly identify what [teacher] candidates should learn (e.g., prep programs should teach phonemic awareness, why this area is important for children's reading development and attainment of the alphabetic principle, what common patterns are in the development of phonemic awareness, specific goals of instruction such as blending and segmentation, and how to assess students' phonemic awareness).

- Hold programs accountable for implementation of scientifically based reading instruction.

- Require a reading licensure test aligned with scientifically based reading instruction for all elementary teachers to earn licensure, and publish pass rates.

- Deploy comprehensive strategy to implement scientifically based reading instruction and prioritize teacher prep.[200]

Many of these recommendations are addressed in California State Assemblymember Blanca Rubio's legislation, AB 2222, discussed in Chapter 7.

For example, her bill requires the California State Board of Education to ensure that all instructional materials adopted "adhere to the science of reading." Also, the bill requires the California Commission on Teacher Credentialing to update its standards and expectations to include "adherence to the science of reading."[201]

Importantly for parents, NCTQ urges: "Use your voice! Ask questions and advocate to ensure scientifically based reading instruction is used in local schools." Specifically, the report recommends:

- Advocate for adoption—both at the district and state levels—of curricula (including core curricula, intervention programs, and supplemental materials) that provide systematic and explicit reading instruction to teach the five components of scientifically based reading instruction. If they exist, call for the removal of low-quality curricula from classrooms, such as those based in balanced literacy, leveled readers, or the use of three-cueing. Share these resources on scientifically based reading instruction with state legislators so they understand the importance of curricula as a help or hindrance in quality reading instruction.

- Advocate for local schools to focus on teachers who are well prepared and committed to scientifically based reading instruction.[202]

California mom Rebeka Sinclair has underscored these principles: "We need more accountability in our education system and we also need more parents to get very involved at the local level, analyzing curriculum as it's adopted by school boards, and not being afraid to ask questions and understanding the reason for making these purchases and the reason for teaching these foundational skills in this way."

Although focused on reading, many of these recommendations can be applicable to math using the science of math, Sugi Sorensen's list of effective math practices, and other evidence-based math resources.

Grassroots pressure is starting to force school districts to be accountable for the academic outcomes of their students.

In San Francisco, parents upset at the ultra-progressive political focus of the city school board, recalled three board members. The new board has committed to spending half of every school board meeting on discussing improving student outcomes.[203]

Also, through a lawsuit and a ballot measure, San Francisco parents have been successful in forcing the school district to re-introduce algebra in the eighth grade.

In Oakland, Kimi Kean of Families in Action says that the next step will be to hold the district and school board accountable to ensure they remain focused on student achievement. "For too long," she said, "generationally failing Black and brown families has been the status quo in our city."[204]

Oakland school board member Jorge Lerma, an ally of Families in Action who is pushing for the board to focus on student achievement, said: "This is call for excellence. We're ready to raise the battle flag."[205]

The parents, teachers, and policymakers featured in this book are ready to raise the battle flag to improve the achievement and learning of children. They have laid out plans of action. And as the parents in San Francisco and Oakland have demonstrated, reform can occur when the grassroots unite to force change on a system that all too often focuses on adult agendas rather than the achievement and needs of children.

As Stephisha Ycoy-Walton emphasized, "I believe as a parent we're responsible for micromanaging our students' education."[206]

"Teachers have unions," Assemblymember Rubio noted, but "students do not."

"We are the only ones that have to advocate for the kids."

ENDNOTES

1   "Scores decline in NAEP reading at grades 4 and 8 compared to 2019," National Assessment for Educational Progress, 2022, available at https://www.nationsreportcard.gov/highlights/reading/2022/

2   Ibid.

3   Ibid.

4   "Largest score declines in NAEP mathematics at grades 4 and 8 since initial assessments in 1990," National Assessment for Educational Progress, 2022, available at https://www.nationsreportcard.gov/highlights/mathematics/2022/

5   Ibid.

6   Ibid.

7   "Teacher Prep Review: Strengthening Elementary Reading Instruction," National Council on Teacher Quality, June 2023, p. 3, available at https://www.nctq.org/dmsView/Teacher_Prep_Review_Strengthening_Elementary_Reading_Instruction

8   Doug Lemov, "Your Neighborhood School is a National Security Risk," *Education Next*, Vol. 24, No. 1, available at https://www.educationnext.org/your-neigh-

borhood-school-national-security-risk-student-achieve-
ment-merit-losing-prospects-era-everybody-wins/

9 Ibid.

10 "A personalized learning resource for all ages," Khan Academy, available at https://www.khanacademy.org/about

11 Ibid.

12 Ibid.

13 Khan Academy Introduces New Mastery Learning Features,"
Khan Academy, available at https://www.prnewswire.com/
news-releases/khan-academy-introduces-new-mastery-learn-
ing-features-300708027.html

14 "Confused by Common Core math? Here's the thinking
behind it," *Washington Post*, March 19, 2021, available at
https://www.washingtonpost.com/lifestyle/2021/03/19/par-
ents-confused-common-core-math

15 Ibid.

16 Ibid.

17 "The Domino Effect," Scott Carrell and Mark Hoestra, *Education Next*. Vol. 9, No. 3, available at https://www.educa-
tionnext.org/domino-effect-2/

18 Ibid.

19 Ibid.

20 "The Sandstorm: Inflated Grades, Increasing Graduation
Rates, and Deflated Test Scores," Larry Sand, For Kids &
Country, January 16, 2024, available at https://www.forkid-
sandcountry.org/blog/the-sandstorm-a-fail-of-two-cities-
copy/#none

21 Ibid.

22 "Saxon Math Review," Smarter Learning Guide, available at
https://smarterlearningguide.com/saxon-math-review/

23 Ibid.

24 "National Reading Panel," National Institute of Child Health
and Human Development, see https://www.nichd.nih.gov/

research/supported/nrp

25 "Teacher Prep Review: Strengthening Elementary Reading Instruction," op. cit,

26 Ibid.

27 Ibid, p. 5.

28 Ibid.

29 Ibid, p. 9.

30 Ibid.

31 Cortney Dilgard, Tracey Hodges, Julianne Coleman, "Phonics Instruction in Early Literacy: Examining Professional Learning, Instructional Resources, and Intervention Intensity," *Reading Psychology*, 2022, Vol. 43, No. 8, p. 542, available at https://www.researchgate.net/publication/363753163_Phonics_Instruction_in_Early_Literacy_Examining_Professional_Learning_Instructional_Resources_and_Intervention_Intensity

32 "Teacher Prep Review: Strengthening Elementary Reading Instruction," op. cit., p. 10.

33 Ibid, p. 11.

34 Ibid, p. 15.

35 Ibid, p. 18.

36 Ibid, p. 35.

37 Ibid, p. 69.

38 Ibid, p. 68.

39 Ibid.

40 "Foundational Skills to Support Reading Understanding in Kindergarten Through 3rd Grade," What Works Clearinghouse, available at https://ies.ed.gov/ncee/WWC/Docs/PracticeGuide/wwc_found_reading_summary_051517.pdf

41 Ibid.

42 Ibid.

43 Ibid.

44 Emily Hanford, "At a Loss for Words," *APM Reports*, August 22, 2019, available at https://www.apmreports.org/episode/2019/08/22/whats-wrong-how-schools-teach-reading

45 "Hundreds of NYC elementary schools used a Teachers College reading curriculum Banks said 'has not worked,'" *Chalkbeat*, February 14, 2023, available at https://www.chalkbeat.org/newyork/2023/2/14/23598611/nyc-schools-reading-instruction-teachers-college-lucy-calkins-balanced-literacy-david-banks/

46 Ibid.

47 "Teacher Prep Review: Strengthening Elementary Reading Instruction," op. cit., p. 69.

48 Ibid.

49 Emily Hanford, op. cit.

50 Emily Hanford and Christopher Peak, "Influential authors Fountas and Pinnell stand behind disproven reading theory," *APM Reports*, November 19, 2021, available at https://www.apmreports.org/story/2021/11/19/fountas-pinnell-disproven-childrens-reading-theory

51 Ibid.

52 Ibid.

53 Ibid.

54 "Summary of Alignment & Usability: Fountas & Pinnell Classroom," EdReports, November 9, 2021, available at https://www.edreports.org/reports/overview/fountas-pinnell-classroom-2020

55 Ibid.

56 Ibid.

57 Ibid.

58 Ibid.

59 Ibid.

60 "Key elements of effective scope and sequence," Reading Rockets, available at https://www.readingrockets.org/class-

room/scope-and-sequence

61 "There are many remedial programs superior to Reading Recovery," *The Conversation*, April 1, 2015, available at https://theconversation.com/there-are-many-remedial-programs-superior-to-reading-recovery-39574

62 "Concerns Raised Over Reading Recovery's Long-Term Effects," *Education Week*, April 29, 2022, available at https://www.edweek.org/teaching-learning/surprise-finding-suggests-reading-recovery-hurts-students-in-the-long-run/2022/04

63 Ibid.

64 "Strengthening Elementary Reading Instruction," op. cit, p. 70.

65 "Dyslexia," Mayo Clinic, available at https://www.mayoclinic.org/diseases-conditions/dyslexia/symptoms-causes/syc-20353552

66 "What Is Structured Literacy," International Dyslexia Association, available at https://dyslexiaida.org/what-is-structured-literacy/

67 Ibid.

68 Ibid.

69 "Teacher Prep Review: Strengthening Elementary Reading Instruction," op. cit., p. 69.

70 "What is the Orton-Gillingham Approach?," Orton-Gillingham Academy, available at https://www.ortonacademy.org/resources/what-is-the-orton-gillingham-approach/

71 Ibid.

72 Ibid.

73 Ibid.

74 See "Teaching Children to Read: An Evidence-Based Assessment of the Scientific Research Literature on Reading and Its Implications for Reading Instruction," National Reading Panel, April 2000, available at https://www.nichd.nih.gov/sites/default/files/publications/pubs/nrp/documents/report.

pdf

75 "English Language Learners and the Five Essential Components of Reading Instruction," Reading Rockets, available at https://www.readingrockets.org/topics/english-language-learners/articles/english-language-learners-and-five-essential-components

76 See https://nces.ed.gov/nationsreportcard/subject/publications/stt2022/pdf/2023010OR8.pdf

77 See https://phono-graphix.com/about_the_method.php

78 "Teachers College to 'Dissolve' Lucy Calkins' Reading and Writing Project," *Education Week*, September 5, 2023, available at https://www.edweek.org/teaching-learning/teachers-college-to-dissolve-lucy-calkins-reading-and-writing-project/2023/09

79 "New Curriculum Review Gives Failing Marks to Two Popular Reading Programs," *Education Week*, November 9, 2021, available at https://www.edweek.org/teaching-learning/new-curriculum-review-gives-failing-marks-to-popular-early-reading-programs/2021/11

80 Christopher Peak, "Benchmark Assessment System reading test is widely used and often wrong," *APM Reports*, December 11, 2023, available at https://www.apmreports.org/story/2023/12/11/benchmark-assessment-system-reading-test-often-wrong

81 Ibid.

82 Ibid.

83 Ibid.

84 Ibid.

85 Ibid.

86 Ibid.

87 Ibid.

88 Ibid.

89 Ibid.

90 Ibid.

91 Ibid.

92 See https://legiscan.com/CA/text/AB2222/id/2919367

93 Ibid.

94 See https://nces.ed.gov/nationsreportcard/subject/publications/stt2022/pdf/2023010CA4.pdf

95 See https://legiscan.com/CA/text/AB2222/id/2919367

96 Ibid.

97 Ibid.

98 Ibid.

99 Ibid.

100 Ibid.

101 Ibid.

102 Ibid.

103 "Strengthening California's Implementation of the Science of Reading through Teacher Preparation," National Council on Teacher Quality, available at https://www.nctq.org/dmsView/California_Profile_-_TeacherPrepReviewReading

104 Ibid.

105 Ibid.

106 Ibid.

107 "NAACP, Children's Defense Fund, and Other State-Wide Advocacy Organizations Join in Support of Assemblywoman Rubio's AB 2222," Office of Assemblymember Blanca Rubio, March 7, 2024, available at https://a48.asmdc.org/press-releases/20240307-naacp-childrens-defense-fund-and-other-state-wide-advocacy-organizations

108 See https://edsource.org/wp-content/uploads/2024/04/EarllyLit-AB2222-CTA-no-032824.pdf

109 "Bill to mandate 'science of reading' in California schools faces teacher union opposition," *EdSource*, April 5, 2024, available at https://edsource.org/2024/bill-to-mandate-sci-

ence-of-reading-in-california-schools-faces-teachers-union-opposition/709193

110 Courtney Dilgard, Tracey Hodges, and Julianne Coleman, op. cit.

111 Ibid.

112 "Bill to mandate 'science of reading' in California class-rooms dies," *EdSource*, April 12, 2024, see https://edsource. org/2024/bill-to-mandate-science-of-reading-in-califor-nia-classrooms-dies/709717?emci=6ec2c7ae-fef8-ee11-aaf0-7c1e52017038&emdi=894338c1-1df9-ee11-aaf0-7c1e52017038&ceid=898703

113 Theodor Rebarber, "The Common Core Debacle," Pioneer Institute, April 2020, p. 10, available at https://files.eric. ed.gov/fulltext/ED604651.pdf

114 Ibid.

115 Ibid, p. 12.

116 Ibid, p. 13.

117 Mengli Song, Rui Yang, and Michael Garet, "Effects of States' Adoption of College- and Career-Ready Standards on Student Achievement," Center on Standards, Alignment, Instruction, and Learning, April 1, 2019, p. 24, available at https://www.c-sail.org/publications/effects-states'-adoption-college-and-career-ready-standards-student-achievement

118 Ibid.

119 Mengli Song, "Did Common Core Standards Work? New Study Finds Small but Disturbing Negative Impacts on Students Academic Achievement," *The 74*, June 4, 2019, available at https://www.the74million.org/article/song-did-common-core-standards-work-new-study-finds-small-but-disturbing-negative-impacts-on-students-academic-achieve-ment/

120 Ibid.

121 "Nearly a decade later, did Common Core work? New research offers clues," *Chalkbeat*, April 29, 2019, available at

https://www.chalkbeat.org/posts/us/2019/04/29/common-core-work-research/

122 Erin Tuttle and J.R. Wilson, "Common Does Not Equal Excellent," American Principles Project, January 2016, available at https://www.chalkbeat.org/posts/us/2019/04/29/common-core-work-research/

123 Ibid, p. 9.

124 Ibid.

125 Ibid, p. 13.

126 Ibid, p. 14.

127 Ibid, p. 16.

128 Ibid.

129 Ibid, p. 22.

130 Ibid, p. 19.

131 Ibid.

132 Williamson Evers and Ze'ev Wurman, "California's Common Core Mistake," Hoover Institution, May 9, 2018, available at https://www.hoover.org/research/californias-common-core-mistake

133 Ibid.

134 Ibid.

135 Ibid.

136 Ibid.

137 Ibid.

138 Ibid.

139 Ibid.

140 "Math wars return to San Francisco amid lawsuit and new Stanford study," *San Francisco Chronicle*, March 21, 2023, available at https://www.sfchronicle.com/bayarea/article/sfusd-algebra-math-wars-stanford-study-17851567.php

141 Ibid.

142 "In the Battle Over Early Algebra, Parents Are Winning," *Wall Street Journal*, February 4, 2024, available at https://www.wsj.com/us-news/education/in-the-battle-over-early-algebra-parents-are-winning-9f52ea5f

143 "Ahead of the Game? Course-Taking Patterns under Math Pathways Reform," Brown University Education Working Paper No. 23-734, March 2023, available at https://edworkingpapers.com/sites/default/files/ai23-734.pdf

144 "San Fran Ballot Measure Reflects 10-Year Battle to Reinstate 8th-Grade Algebra," *The 74*, March 4, 2024, available at https://www.yahoo.com/news/san-fran-ballot-measure-reflects-173000981.html

145 "San Francisco Voters Overwhelmingly Support Algebra's Return to 8th Grade," *The 74*, March 6, 2024, available at https://www.the74million.org/article/san-fran-voters-overwhelmingly-support-algebras-return-to-8th-grade/

146 See https://www.thescienceofmath.com

147 See https://www.thescienceofmath.com/what-is-math-proficiency

148 See https://www.thescienceofmath.com/what-is-explicit-instruction

149 See https://www.thescienceofmath.com/misconceptions-inquiry-based-versus-explicit-instruction

150 See https://www.thescienceofmath.com/misconceptions-conceptual-procedural

151 See https://www.thescienceofmath.com/misconceptions-productive-struggle-causes-more-robust-understanding-and-learning

152 See https://www.thescienceofmath.com/timed-tests-cause-math-anxiety

153 See Lance Izumi, Vicki Murray, and Rachel Chaney, *Not as Good as You Think: Why the Middle Class Needs School Choice* (San Francisco: Pacific Research Institute, 2007), available at https://www.amazon.com/Not-Good-You-Think-Middle/dp/1934276065

154 Matthew Clavel, "How Not to Teach Math," *City Journal*, March 7, 2003, available at https://www.city-journal.org/article/how-not-to-teach-math

155 Ibid.

156 Ibid.

157 Ibid.

158 See https://pamath2009.wordpress.com/everyday-math-what-is-it/

159 Ibid.

160 Tom Loveless, "The Use and Misuse of Research in Educational Reform," in *Education Policy 1998*, Diane Ravitch, ed. (Washington, DC: Brookings Institution Press, 1998): pp. 285-86.

161 See https://wrt120.digitalwcu.org/wp-content/uploads/2017/09/freire.pdf

162 Tom Loveless, op. cit.

163 Sugi Sorensen, "Thoughts on Effective Mathematics," *Cryptomeric Thoughts*, July 13, 2023, available at https://sugisorensen.substack.com/p/thoughts-on-effective-math-instruction

164 Ibid.

165 David Kristofferson, "Pros and Cons of the CPM Textbook Series," *EduIssues*, August 18, 2017, available at https://eduissues.com/2017/08/28/pros-and-cons-of-the-cpm-math-textbook-series/

166 Ibid.

167 Ibid.

168 Ibid.

169 Ibid.

170 Ibid.

171 Ibid.

172 Ibid.

173 Ibid.

174 Ibid.

175 Ibid.

176 See https://beastacademy.com

177 See https://www.mathlearningcenter.org/curriculum/bridges-mathematics

178 Ibid.

179 See https://www.edglossary.org/direct-instruction/

180 Gillian Kidman, "Explainer: what is inquiry-based learning and how does it prepare children for the real world," *The Conversation*, April 30, 2014, available at https://theconversation.com/explainer-what-is-inquiry-based-learning-and-how-does-it-help-prepare-children-for-the-real-world-115299

181 Ibid.

182 Ibid.

183 Ze'ev Wurman and Williamson Evers, "California's math framework lacks sound research evidence to justify its progressive agenda," *EdSource*, April 18, 2022, available at https://edsource.org/2022/californias-math-framework-lacks-research-to-justify-its-progressive-agenda/670470

184 Richard Clark, Paul Kirschner, and John Sweller, "Putting Students on the Path to Learning," *American Educator*, Spring 2012, p. 7, available at https://files.eric.ed.gov/fulltext/EJ971752.pdf

185 Ibid.

186 Ibid, p. 8.

187 Ibid.

188 Ibid.

189 Ibid.

190 Ibid, p. 6.

191 "Furious Oakland parents are declaring war on politics and status quo in schools: 'This is a call for excellence,'"

San Francisco Chronicle, March 28, 2024, available at https://www.sfchronicle.com/bayarea/article/oakland-parents-schools-19367308.php

192 See http://www.ed-data.org/district/Alameda/Oakland-Unified

193 Ibid.

194 "Furious Oakland parents are declaring war on politics and status quo in schools: 'This is a call for excellence,'" op. cit.

195 Ibid.

196 Ibid.

197 Ibid.

198 Ibid.

199 "Teacher Prep Review: Strengthening Elementary Reading Instruction," op. cit., pp. 43-44.

200 Ibid, pp. 40-41.

201 See https://legiscan.com/CA/text/AB2222/id/2919367

202 "Teacher Prep Review: Strengthening Elementary Reading Instruction," op. cit., p. 45.

203 "Furious Oakland parents are declaring war on politics and status quo in schools: 'This is a call for excellence,'" op. cit.

204 Ibid.

205 Ibid.

206 Ibid.

AUTHOR BIOGRAPHY

Lance Izumi is Senior Director of the Center for Education at the Pacific Research Institute. He has written and produced books, studies, and films on a wide variety of education topics. Most recently, he is the author of the 2023 book *The Great Parent Revolt: How Parents and Grassroots Leaders Are Fighting Critical Race Theory in America's Schools* and the 2022 book *The Homeschool Boom: Pandemic, Policies, and Possibilities*.

He is a former two-term president of the Board of Governors of the California Community Colleges, the largest system of higher education in the nation, and served as a member of the Board from 2004 to 2015.

He served two terms as chair of the Board of Directors of the Foundation for California Community Colleges.

Lance served as a commissioner on the California Postsecondary Education Commission and as a member of the United States Civil Rights Commission's California Advisory Committee.

Lance received his Juris Doctorate from the University of Southern California School of Law, his Master of Arts in political science from the University of California at Davis, and his Bachelor of Arts in economics and history from the University of California at Los Angeles.

ACKNOWLEDGMENTS

Many people assisted in the preparation of this book. The author would like to especially thank McKenzie Richards who provided invaluable research and organizational assistance to this project. Also, he would like to thank Rebecca Friedrichs and Wenyuan Wu for their interviewee recommendations.

In addition, the author would like to thank Pacific Research Institute president and CEO Sally Pipes for her leadership and support of this project. Also, he thanks PRI COO Rowena Itchon and PRI vice president of marketing and communications Tim Anaya for editing the book (any remaining errors and omissions are the sole responsibility of the author). Thanks also go to graphic designer Dana Beigel, PRI vice president of development Ben Smithwick, and the other dedicated staff who made this book possible.

The author of this book worked independently and his views and conclusions do not necessarily represent those of the board, supporters, and staff of PRI.

ABOUT PACIFIC RESEARCH INSTITUTE

The Pacific Research Institute (PRI) champions freedom, opportunity, and personal responsibility by advancing free-market policy solutions. It provides practical solutions for the policy issues that impact the daily lives of all Americans, and demonstrates why the free market is more effective than the government at providing the important results we all seek: good schools, quality health care, a clean environment, and a robust economy.

Founded in 1979 and based in San Francisco, PRI is a non-profit, non-partisan organization supported by private contributions. Its activities include publications, public events, media commentary, community leadership, legislative testimony, and academic outreach.

Center for Business and Economics
PRI shows how the entrepreneurial spirit—the engine of economic growth and opportunity—is stifled by onerous taxes, regulations, and lawsuits. It advances policy reforms that promote a robust economy, consumer choice, and innovation.

Center for Education
PRI works to restore to all parents the basic right to choose the best educational opportunities for their children. Through research and grassroots outreach, PRI promotes parental choice in education, high academic standards, teacher quality, charter schools, and school-finance reform.

Center for the Environment
PRI reveals the dramatic and long-term trend toward a cleaner, healthier environment. It also examines and promotes the essential ingredients for abundant resources and environmental quality: property rights, markets, local action, and private initiative.

Center for Health Care
PRI demonstrates why a single-payer Canadian model would be detrimental to the health care of all Americans. It proposes market-based reforms that would improve affordability, access, quality, and consumer choice.

Center for California Reform
The Center for California Reform seeks to reinvigorate California's entrepreneurial self-reliant traditions. It champions solutions in education, business, and the environment that work to advance prosperity and opportunity for all the state's residents.

Center for Medical Economics and Innovation
The Center for Medical Economics and Innovation aims to educate policymakers, regulators, health care professionals, the media, and the public on the critical role that new technologies play in improving health and accelerating economic growth.

Free Cities Center
The Free Cities Center cultivates innovative ideas to improve our cities and urban life based around freedom and property rights – not government.